A Review of Social Economy Resear

Voluntaristics Review

Volumes published in this Brill Research Perspectives title are listed at *brill.com/vrbr*

A Review of Social Economy Research in Canada

By

Laurie Mook and Jack Quarter

BRILL

LEIDEN | BOSTON

Originally published as Volume 3(4) 2018, in *Voluntaristics Review*, DOI:10.1163/24054933-12340025.

ICSERA is a global infrastructure organization, research-information institute, and umbrella association for voluntaristics (nonprofit, third sector) researcher associations (www.icsera.org). A Florida-based, IRS-501(c)(3) nonprofit 2010+, the International Council of Voluntarism, Civil Society, and Social Economy Researcher Associations officially sponsors *Voluntaristics Review* and the *Palgrave Handbook of Volunteering, Civic Participation, and Nonprofit Associations*.

Library of Congress Control Number: 2019930469

Typeface for the Latin, Greek, and Cyrillic scripts: "Brill". See and download: brill.com/brill-typeface.

ISBN 978-90-04-39860-3 (paperback)
ISBN 978-90-04-39861-0 (e-book)

This book is printed on acid-free paper and produced in a sustainable manner.

Contents

A Review of Social Economy Research in Canada

Laurie Mook
Arizona State University
lmook@asu.edu

Jack Quarter
University of Toronto
jack.quarter@utoronto.ca

Abstract

Canada is a federal parliamentary democracy, officially bilingual (English and French), and one of the most multicultural countries in the world. Indeed, more than one-fifth of Canada's population consists of first-generation immigrants, and a similar percentage classify themselves as visible minorities. According to the 2016 census there are more than 250 distinct ethnic origins, often with distinct languages (Statistics Canada, 2016, 2017a). A confederation of ten provinces and three territories, Canada has a current population of over 36 million people who live across an expansive geographic area that constitutes the second largest country in the world. Most of its population live in urban settings (83%), with the largest cities being Toronto, Montreal and Vancouver (Statistics Canada, 2017b). Toronto is classified as the third-most cosmopolitan city in the world following Dubai and Brussels (World Atlas, 2018).

In this multifaceted context, the social economy of Canada plays an important role in bridging the public and private sectors to form a strong social infrastructure (Quarter, Mook, & Armstrong, 2018). It constitutes a vast range of organizations guided by social objectives including nonprofit organizations such as charities, foundations, and social enterprises; and cooperatives both non-financial, in fields such as housing, childcare, healthcare, and farm marketing, and financial such as credit unions and caisses populaires.

There are distinct traditions of the social economy in anglophone and francophone parts of Canada. There are also traditions specific to particular populations, such as the Black social economy (Hossein, 2013); and the Indigenous social economy (Restoule, Gruner, & Metatawabin, 2012; Sengupta, Vieta, & McMurtry, 2015; Wuttunee, 2010). In this review, we look at the anglophone research on the social economy, noting that there are also French-language research institutions and educational programs focusing on the social economy; however, a review of these is beyond the scope of this paper.

After providing an overview of the concept of the social economy in Canada, we go on to summarize research on its scope and size in the Canadian context. Using a Venn diagram, we highlight the interactions between the different sectors in society and emphasize that the social economy is an integral part of a mixed economy that serves in many ways as its social infrastructure. We find four different types of social economy organizations: social economy businesses, community economic development organizations, public sector nonprofits, and civil society organizations. From there, we focus on voluntaristic behaviors of giving, volunteering (formal and informal), and participating. Our focus shifts to describing the infrastructure supporting research of the sector, including key academic and umbrella associations and networks, as well as formal and informal education programs. Finally, we describe key funders of social economy research including government and foundations.

Keywords

social economy – nonprofit organizations – charities – cooperatives – credit unions – foundations – social enterprises – formal volunteering – informal volunteering – participating – Canada

Editor's Introduction: Social Economy or the Solidarity Economy as Part of Nonprofit Sector Economics

The present issue of *Voluntaristics Review, VR* 3.4, surveys research on the social economy in English-speaking Canada. Economists have been interested in the social aspects of the economy since early in the 20th century and even earlier, and sociologists and other social scientists have joined them. For instance, the quarterly academic journal, *Annals of Public, Social, and Cooperative Economics*, was founded in 1908 (cf., Smith, 2013, p. 645), and the quarterly journal, *Industrial & Labor Relations Review*, was founded in the mid-20th-century, in 1947 (op. cit., p. 646). The *International Journal of Social Economics* was founded in 1973. The *Canadian Journal of Nonprofit and Social Economy Research* was founded in 2010 (www.anserj.ca). Sometimes the term *solidarity economy* is substituted for *social economy*, and in Spanish the term *otra economia* may be substituted (see www.riless.org).

Several social economy researcher associations have been formed in the past eighty years. The *global* Association for Social Economics/ASE was organized in 1941 (op. cit., p. 646); the Research Network for Social Enterprise (mostly European region, but now global) was founded in 1996 (www.emes .net); the *world region* "Red de Investigadores Latinoamericanos de Economía Social y Solidaria"/RILESS (in Spanish; translated into English as "Network of Latin American Researchers on Social and Solidarity Economy) was founded in 2000 (op. cit., p. 643; www.riless.org); and the "Réseau Inter-Universitaire de l'Economie Sociale et Solidaire" (in French; translated into English as "Inter-University Network of the Social and Solidarity Economy") was founded in 2015, with mostly French universities, but also other European universities (www.riuess.org).

Various *national* social economy researcher associations have also been formed in the past two decades: Association for the Development of Documentation on the Social Economy/ADDES in France in the 1990s (www .addes.asso.fr; op. cit., p. 646); Association for Nonprofit and Social Economy Research Canada/ANSER-ARES in 2007 (www.anser-ares.ca; op. cit., p. 641); Canadian Association for Studies in Cooperation (www.coopresearch.coop). Earlier, the UK Society for Cooperative Studies was formed in the 1960s (www.co-opstudies; op. cit., p. 643).

In addition to various major academic journals and researcher associations focused on social economy, many books have been published, especially since 1990, on social economy and related topics (e.g., Amin, 2009; Bouchard, 2009, 2013; CIRIEC, 2007; Defourny, Hulgård, & Pestoff, 2014; McMurtry, 2010; Mook, Quarter, & Ryan, 2012; Mook et al., 2015; Quarter, Mook, & Armstrong, 2018; Yunus, 2010). Sundry key articles and book chapters on social economy have also been published (e.g., Vieta et al., 2016). Related books, journal articles, and book chapters have been published on nonprofit economics in general (e.g., Seaman & Young, 2018) and social entrepreneurship (e.g., Guo & Bielefeld, 2014).

Thus, in addition to being a sub-field of economics, the social economy or solidarity economy is an established sub-field of voluntaristics, as the global field and emergent academic discipline of nonprofit sector and voluntary action research (see Smith, 2013, 2016). For some academics and scholars, *social economy* is a full synonym for *voluntaristics*, nonprofit/third sector studies, or civil society studies. Either way, all aspects of the social economy are relevant to this journal, especially the present review of social economy research in English-speaking Canada.

David Horton Smith, Ph.D. (Harvard)
Editor-in-Chief, Voluntaristics Review

Research and Emeritus Professor of Sociology, Boston College, Chestnut Hill,
MA, USA
Honorary Visiting Research Professor, Centre for Studies of Civil Society and
the Nonprofit Sector, National Research University Higher School of
Economics, Moscow, Russian Federation
Honorary Visiting Professor, School of Arts and Sciences, City, University of
London, London, UK
Visiting Scholar, NGO Research Center and Institute for Philanthropy,
Tsinghua University, Beijing, China

References

Amin, A. (Ed.). (2009). *Social economy: International perspectives on economic solidarity*. London: Zed Press.

Avila, R. C., & Monzon, J. L. (2012). *The social economy in the European Union*. N°. CESE/COMM/05/2005. The European Economic and Social Committee (EESC). Brussels, Belgium: CIRIEC INTERNATIONAL.

Bouchard, M. J. (Ed.). (2013). *Innovation and the social economy: The Quebec experience*. Toronto: University of Toronto Press.

Bouchard, M. J. (Ed.) (2009). *The worth of the social economy: An international perspective*. Brussels: P.I.E.-Peter Lang.

Defourny, J., Hulgård, L., & Pestoff, V. (Eds). (2014). *Social enterprise and the third sector. Changing European landscapes in a comparative perspective*. London: Routledge.

Guo, C. & Bielefeld, W. (2014). *Social entrepreneurship: An evidence-based approach to creating social value*. San Francisco, CA: Jossey-Bass.

McMurtry, J. J. (Ed.). (2010). *Living economics: Canadian perspectives on the social economy, co-operatives, and community economic development*. Toronto: Edmond Montgomery Press.

Mook, L., Quarter, J., & Ryan, S. (Eds). (2012). *Researching the social economy*. Toronto: University of Toronto Press.

Mook, L., Whitman, J. R., Quarter, J., & Armstrong, A. (2015). *Understanding the social economy of the United States*. Toronto: University of Toronto Press.

Quarter, J., Mook, L., & Armstrong, A. (2018). *Understanding the social economy: A Canadian perspective*, 2nd ed. Toronto: University of Toronto Press.

Seaman, B. A. & Young, D. R. (Eds). (2018). *Handbook of research on nonprofit economics and management*, 2nd ed. Northampton, MA: Edward Elgar Publishing.

Smith, D. H. (2013). "Growth of research associations and journals in the emerging discipline of altruistics." *Nonprofit and Voluntary Sector Quarterly, 42*(4), 638–656.

Smith, D. H. (2016). "A survey of voluntaristics: Research on the growth of the global, interdisciplinary, socio-behavioral science field and emergent *inter-discipline*." *Voluntaristics Review, 1*(2), 1–81.

Vieta, M., Quarter, J., Spear, R., & Moskovskaya, A. (2016). "Participation in worker cooperatives." In D. H. Smith, R. A. Stebbins, & J. Grotz (Eds), *The Palgrave handbook of volunteering, civic participation, and nonprofit associations* (pp. 436–453). Basingstoke: Palgrave Macmillan.

Yunus, M. (2010). *Building social business: The new kind of capitalism that serves humanity's most pressing needs*. New York: Public Affairs.

Introduction

Canada is a federal parliamentary democracy, officially bilingual (English and French), and one of the most multicultural countries in the world. Indeed, more than one-fifth of Canada's population consists of first-generation immigrants, and a similar percentage classify themselves as visible minorities. According to the 2016 census there are more than 250 distinct ethnic origins, often with distinct languages (Statistics Canada, 2016, 2017a). A confederation of ten provinces and three territories, Canada has a current population of over 36 million people who live across an expansive geographic area that constitutes the second largest country in the world. Most of its population live in urban settings (83%), with the largest cities being Toronto, Montreal and Vancouver (Statistics Canada, 2017b). Toronto is classified as the third-most cosmopolitan city in the world following Dubai and Brussels (World Atlas, 2017).

In this multifaceted context, the social economy of Canada plays an important role in bridging the public and private sectors to form a strong social infrastructure (Quarter, Mook, & Armstrong, 2018). It constitutes a vast range of organizations guided by social objectives including nonprofit organizations such as charities, foundations, and social enterprises; and cooperatives both non-financial, in fields such as housing, childcare, healthcare, and farm marketing, and financial, such as credit unions and caisses populaires.

There are distinct traditions of the social economy in anglophone and francophone parts of Canada. There are also traditions specific to particular populations, such as the Black social economy (Hossein, 2013); and the Indigenous social economy (Restoule, Gruner, & Metatawabin, 2012; Sengupta, Vieta, & McMurtry, 2015; Wuttunee, 2010). In this review, we look at the anglophone research on the social economy, focusing particularly on the 21st century. We start by providing an overview of the concept of social economy, and go on in Part 2 to summarize research on its scope and size in the Canadian context. From there, we focus on voluntaristic behaviors of giving, volunteering, and participating in Part 3. Our focus shifts in Part 4 to describing the infrastructure supporting research of the sector, including key academic and umbrella associations and networks, as well as formal and informal education programs. We also describe key funders of social economy research including government and foundations. We conclude with a summary in Part 5.

1   The Social Economy Concept

1.1   *The Rise of the Social Economy Concept*
In a short paper it is challenging to do proper service to the differing conceptions of the social economy. Some approaches are very selective; others, such as ours, are broader and more inclusive. We shall provide some select examples, then turn to our framework.

The differing interpretations of the social economy could be grouped into those that focus on distinct forms of organization (nonprofits, cooperatives, credit unions, and mutual associations) and those that focus on distinct criteria or norms that differentiate organizations in the social economy from society as a whole (Borzaga & Defourny, 2001; Bouchard, 2013; Spear, 2010).

Some conceptions of the social economy privilege market activities and focus on what we label as either *social economy businesses* (SEBS) or *social enterprises* (see, e.g., Borzaga & Defourny, 2001; Borzaga & Depedri, 2009; Defourny, Hulgård, & Pestoff, 2014; Defourny & Monzón Campos, 1992). We believe that it is inappropriate to privilege market activities in reference to the social economy, as there are many examples of organizations making important contributions to society that do not sell their services in the market yet generate economic value, either explicitly as through the purchase of supplies or implicitly in the imputed market value of their services. Indeed, much research has illustrated the economic value of volunteers (see, e.g., Mook, 2013; Mook, Quarter, & Richmond, 2007). Even though volunteers are unpaid labor, they are central to the workforce of the social economy and of critical importance to the broader society. The early 20th century economist Arthur Pigou pointed out the flawed logic of overemphasizing market exchange when he mused that if bachelors en masse married their housekeepers, and assuming that they did the same work but no longer received wages, it would have a negative effect on the gross domestic product. This is known as Pigou's Paradox.

1.2   *The Quebec Tradition via Francophone Europe*
In francophone parts of Europe and in particular those associated with the association CIRIEC (http://www.ciriec.uliege.be/en/), the social economy is seen to include cooperatives (including credit unions), mutual societies and

associations, and social enterprises in general, organizations that operate in the market (CIRIEC, 2007; Monzón Campos & Chaves, 2012). Other forms of nonprofit organizations, such as those without earned revenues and those relying heavily on government funding and influenced in part by government policies, are excluded; this latter group of organizations is labeled as *public sector nonprofits* within our framework.

The francophone European tradition was picked up in Quebec, where le Chantier de l'économie sociale is the apex organization for the social economy (Mendell & Neamtan, 2010) and its trust fund (la Fiducie du Chantier de l'économie sociale) has played a vital role in its development. Le Chantier has worked closely with CIRIEC Canada, a network of academics led from the Université du Québec à Montréal (http://www.ciriec.uqam.ca/).

Some argue that the social economy in Quebec has the characteristics of a social movement in that it is based on a broad coalition of organizations and it is impacting government policies (Arsenault, 2018; Favreau, 2006; Mendell & Neamtan, 2010; Mendell & Rouzier, 2006). A social movement perspective is reflected in the statement adopted in 2006 at the Social and Solidarity Economy Summit in Montreal (SSES, 2006, p. 1): "We, actors of the social economy from the community, cooperative and mutual benefit movements and associations, from cultural, environmental and social movements, unions, international cooperation and local and regional development organizations, affirm with pride and determination our commitment to building a social and solidarity economy locally, regionally, nationally and internationally."

The vision is not simply to strengthen organizations in Quebec's social economy but to build a new society "locally, regionally, nationally and internationally." As stated by Quebeckers Shragge and Fontan (2000, p. 9), "A social economy implies a basic reorientation of the whole economy and related institutions."

The European Commission (2015) takes a broader view than the francophone tradition and does not impose the same restrictions on the inclusion of some forms of nonprofit organizations as in francophone Europe and Quebec. As will become apparent, this paper embraces the broader view. We do not treat the social economy as a social movement, but as a unique set of institutions that are part of a broader society and interact with the other parts of society in many ways. Nevertheless, we recognize that within the social economy there are many social movement organizations—both individual and networks—related to many social issues, some broad (such as the environment and gender) and others specific (such as proportional representation and the minimum wage). Within our framework, social movement organizations are labeled within the broader section on civil society organizations.

1.3   *Other Movement Interpretations*

There are some other social movement interpretations of the social economy. Hossein (2013, 2014a, 2014b, 2016) refers to the *Black social economy*, with her focus on informal lending systems in poor areas of Jamaica, Haiti, and Guyana, types of activity that would fit within our conception of civil society. These traditions have also been brought to Canada, for instance, the African Canadian "Banker Ladies" in Montreal and Toronto (Hossein, 2017). Similarly, some research refers to a social economy distinct to Aboriginal or Indigenous communities (Restoule, Gruner, & Metatawabin, 2012; Sengupta, Vieta, & McMurtry, 2015; Wuttunee, 2010). In general, those activities would be covered within our conception of community economic development organizations (CED) and social enterprise. These other interpretations also underline the point that the social economy is in large part a Eurocentric concept, and it may not be applicable to societies that either lack Eurocentric values or that are aspiring to change those values (McMurtry, 2010).

1.4   *The Social Economy as Bridging a Mixed Economy*

Our social economy framework, as outlined in detail in our book, *Understanding the social economy: A Canadian perspective*, is an interactive and systemic approach for understanding the extraordinary varieties of organizations that are guided by their social objectives. It highlights similarities and differences among organizations with social objectives—nonprofits, cooperatives, and social enterprises. These social objectives can be expressed in differing ways. The priority that they give to their social objectives affects how the organization functions; it places constraints on how the organization's property can be used, the disposition of any surplus earnings, and who can benefit from the assets. In contrast to a private sector business, the assets of a social economy organization (SEO) are used to create social wealth for members or the public, not for increasing an individual investor's economic wealth.

We use a Venn diagram both to classify the organizations in the social economy and to present their differing forms of interactions with the private and public sectors. In looking at the components of the social economy—social economy businesses, community economic development organizations, public sector nonprofits, and civil society organizations—we can see the many functions that these organizations serve. In brief, the social economy is an integral part of a mixed economy that serves in many ways as its social infrastructure.

Our approach is dynamic in that the boundaries between the social economy and the private and public sectors are in flux. Different points in time and different contexts will result in different balances among different models of organization that will come and go, and we can expect that such changes will continue well into the future.

1.5 Social Objectives: Central to the Social Economy

The core feature of our conception of organizations in the social economy is that their social objectives are central to their mission: "The social economy bridges the many different types of self-governing organizations that are guided by their social objectives in the goods and services that they offer" (Quarter, Mook, & Armstrong, 2018, p. 4).

Public sector organizations, it could be argued, also prioritize their social objectives, for example, in delivering many social programs (such as Medicare, employment insurance, and public pensions). A fundamental difference, however, is that public sector agencies, unlike organizations in the social economy, are not self-governing. To emphasize the difference from the public sector, nonprofit organizations in the United States are referred to as "private" (Salamon et al., 1999). We prefer the label *social* because private could be confused with private property, whereas social economy organizations are creating social wealth for public benefit. Similarly, it might be argued that private sector firms meet social needs by creating jobs and satisfying consumers. This may be true, but their primary objective is to generate wealth for their owners. Therefore, the organizational dynamic of private sector firms differs from organizations in the social economy.

For social economy organizations, their social objectives are often asserted within a mission statement that may be written into the organization's charter. The social objectives are not a secondary consideration, as when a conventional business decides to embrace corporate social responsibility (CSR) while in pursuit of its primary objective of increasing profit, but are central to the organization's purpose from its inception. Even though social objectives are central to organizations in the social economy, it should be noted that an organization's social commitments may change over time, and even more so in a society undergoing rapid technological change.

Although all organizations in the social economy are guided by their social objectives, these take on a different form depending on whether the organization is pursuing charitable objectives, meeting the needs of a membership, or selling its services in the market. Even within these broad categories, each organization is distinct and contains social objectives that are unique to its purposes.

1.5.1 Charitable Objectives for Public Benefit

A *charitable objective* is one form of social objective. Charitable organizations in the wealthy nations have a long, historical tradition of social giving. Religious charity stems from at least as far back as the Old Testament (Loewenberg, 2001; Robbins, 2006), and the evolution of the legal status of charity in the Western world gained traction in the Middle Ages in England (Hopkins, 1987).

As charitable activities have broadened from their narrow religious base to become more secular, English society attempted to codify the purposes of charitable gifts in the preamble of the Statute of Charitable Uses (or Statute of Elizabeth) of 1601. The list is lengthy but includes "some for aged, impotent and poor people, some for maintenance of sick and maimed soldiers and mariners, schools of learning, free schools, and scholars in universities, some for repair of bridges, ports, havens, causeways, churches" (as cited in Fremont-Smith, 2004, p. 29). The Statute of Elizabeth launched the gradual broadening of the concept of charity in Anglophone nations from its religious roots and from a strict focus on the relief of poverty.

The secularization of charity took on a new urgency because of the Industrial Revolution and the related social problems resulting from people, even children, working in factories for unimaginably lengthy hours by current standards, and living in overcrowded urban slums with poor housing and sanitation. These conditions stimulated the growth of charitable organizations that both offered social services and advocated for improvements in living and working conditions.

From the mid-19th century, several powerful influences came to bear on the development of charities. These included the creation of social work as a profession to assist people in need; the settlement house movement that sought to ease the living conditions of the poor; and the growth of "scientific charity" that departed from a reliance on almsgiving and that led to charity organizations operating apart from government (Kirk & Reid, 2002). One consequence of scientific charity was collaboration between organizations in fundraising and what eventually became the United Way movement and other similar organizations based on religious groups (Martin, 1985).

A profound influence on the development of charitable giving was the wealthy industrialist Andrew Carnegie, who through his pamphlet, *The Gospel of Wealth*, written in 1889, urged the wealthy to abandon the practice of simply passing on their wealth to their family. In a fundamental departure from tradition, Carnegie stated unequivocally that the wealthy should give it all away: "The man who dies thus rich dies disgraced" (Carnegie, 1995 [1889], p. 10). Carnegie's message was blunt, and he set an example by parting with his vast fortune, most of it prior to his death in 1919, on many projects, including libraries that can still be found across Canada. Carnegie, who was paternalistic in his attitude to the poor, argued that the wealthy (who he believed knew best) had an obligation to administer their wealth for the benefit of the public and "to produce the most beneficial results for the community" (p. 9).

Although Carnegie was not the first philanthropist, his philosophy was an important influence on the modern movement of strategic philanthropy in which foundations—representing a portion of the capital of a society's wealthiest—target their revenues to particular social objectives that, in the view of their trustees, represent a public benefit. Carnegie's urging for the wealthy to give it all away, needless to say, has been less influential, though it has been revived, in part, by the more recent challenge of US mega-billionaires Warren Buffet and Bill and Melinda Gates to give away at least 50% of their wealth through the Giving Pledge, and like Carnegie, urging other people of wealth to follow suit (Loomis, 2010).

Today, charitable objectives constitute a broad and heterogeneous mix, but they must pass a public benefit test—for example, they must help with relieving poverty, the advancement of education, the advancement of religion, and/or other purposes beneficial to the community (Canada Revenue Agency, 2015). These objectives have permitted organizations with such functions as international aid, education, youth programs, health care, family services, culture and the arts, and heritage and environmental protection to be classified as having a charitable status. A distinction can thus be made between charity as a community's response to those in dire need and organizations with broader charitable objectives that meet the criteria required for charitable status under the taxation laws, thereby permitting donors to achieve a tax benefit. Although modern charities are of both types, organizations meeting the broader criteria are more commonplace. This change can be called the *universalization of charity*.

The tax benefits granted to organizations with a charitable registration (tax credits to their donors and exemption from tax for the organization, the latter applying not only to organizations with a charitable registration but to non-profits in general) come at a price. Tax-exempt organizations are for public benefit only, and their assets are not the personal property of their members, officers, or employees. Rather, their assets can be viewed as *social property*, belonging neither to private owners nor to government. Even though these organizations are governed by a board of directors or by trustees, their property does not belong to those individuals. If an organization with a charitable registration is closed ("wound up"), its assets are to be transferred for public benefit, normally to another similar nonprofit organization (Carter, Hoffstein, & Parachin, 2016). The trustees or directors of charitable organizations have a fiduciary responsibility to the public (i.e., an ethical duty or relationship of trust) and are not permitted to operate the organization for personal gain. The public benefit characteristic of charitable organizations and other nonprofits makes them attractive to donors and to volunteers whose giving is guided by altruistic motives. Volunteers form their board of directors and may be their primary human resources. In Canada, such board members cannot be compensated.

In spite of the involvement of volunteers and donors, many charitable organizations have substantial income and expenses like businesses in general do. In any given year, their income may exceed their expenses (a surplus), but even under these circumstances their expenditures should be guided by the organization's social objectives. Nonprofit organizations have a "distribution constraint," meaning that if they have an annual surplus they are restricted from distributing dividends to members, employees, and officers, like a business corporation might do for its shareholders (Hansmann, 1980, 1996; Salamon & Anheier, 1997). This constraint is not a guarantee of good conduct, however, as it does not prohibit nonprofit organizations from paying top executives excessively. Typically, surpluses allow nonprofits to invest in improving or expanding their services in ways that are consistent with their social objectives.

1.5.2   Meeting Member Needs through Mutual Aid/Self-Help
Mutual associations are nonprofit organizations whose members come together to satisfy a shared interest or need through a service that the organization offers. Increasingly, mutual associations serve their members online. Some bonds of association that bring people together are a common heritage, occupation, location, religion, profession, health concern, or social interest. Mutual associations are based on mutual aid or self-help, a form of reciprocity that the Russian biologist Peter Kropotkin argued in his classic book, *Mutual aid: A factor of evolution* (1989 [1902]), is critical to human evolution.

Cooperatives are a form of mutual association and embrace the idea of mutual aid, as signified in their definition by the International Cooperative Alliance (ICA), the umbrella organization for cooperatives worldwide. Cooperatives, like mutual aid organizations in general, involve people associating with each other to help themselves.

Self-help organizations, broadly speaking, have their roots among exploited groups in society (MacPherson, 1979). Some of the oldest associations in the New World were mutual benefit societies in which people, often of common religion, ethnocultural heritage, or geographical origin (e.g., a city from which they immigrated to Canada), arranged services (e.g., insurance and burials) for their members. Some examples are the Chinese cemetery in Victoria, set up in 1903 by the Chinese Consolidated Benevolent Association; the North Waterloo Farmers Mutual Fire Insurance Company, organized in 1874 by farmers in Waterloo county in Ontario because of prohibitive rates that they were being charged for insurance; the first credit union in Lévis, Quebec, organized by the pioneers Alphonse and Dorimène Desjardins (their creation has evolved into a major eponymous corporation headquartered in Montreal), so that working people could obtain consumer loans at reasonable rates (MacPherson, 1999); and the Benevolent Irish Society of Prince Edward Island (PEI), established in 1825 to assist Irish immigrants to PEI. Some mutual associations adhere to the tradition of being organized around exploited groups (e.g., a union local or workplace association), but others simply involve a common social interest (e.g., the Historical Society of Alberta), a shared experience (such as by members of the hundreds of Royal Canadian Legion branches who have fought in a war), a marginalized social group (e.g., the Aboriginal Friendship Centres of Saskatchewan), or some other commonality, including a privileged status (such as enjoyed by the members of a golf club or a business association, e.g., the Canada Singapore Business Association). The bonds of association might differ, but such organizations are set up to meet social needs expressed through shared social and cultural objectives.

Mutual associations, like organizations in the social economy in general, are self-governing. Voting rights are accorded based on membership rather than according to property holdings as in profit-oriented businesses (Ellerman, 1990). Basing voting rights on membership is similar to according voting rights to citizenship, as in a political democracy, that is, one citizen, one vote. In the social economy, governance is similar: one member, one vote. In a mutual association, the governance is typically a subset of the members who form the board of directors, or in cases in which there is no formal incorporation, an executive committee. Many mutual associations may have a very broad membership (e.g., the members of a political party or a major union). For others, members of the board or the trustees may be the entire membership, but the organization still should operate according to the principle of one member, one vote.

1.5.3 Operating with Social Objectives in the Market

A third form of social objective is exemplified by organizations operating in the market but guided by their social objectives rather than the business imperative of increasing profits for the owners. Capital invested in profit-oriented businesses, and especially in maturing companies, typically has a very weak social commitment in comparison with the financial imperative to increase shareholder returns. With the exception of small owner-operated enterprises that are tied to a neighborhood or some larger firms that depend on a particular location for their products (e.g., resource extraction), profit-oriented businesses remain loyal to a community only as long as they obtain a competitive rate of return. When a greater return is possible from other investments or from conducting business elsewhere, profit-oriented businesses will shift their loyalties. By comparison, organizations in the social economy not only regard their social objectives as their priority; they also have loyalties to either a defined community or a defined membership. Cooperatives operating in the market as an example, owned and controlled by their members, are less likely to make speculative investments with their own assets; they are also more likely to preserve employment in difficult economic times (Birchall & Ketilson, 2009), a strategy that may reduce the organization's income at year's end.

We use the label social economy business for firms that earn their revenues from the market but that make their social objectives primary. There are different variations of this practice, including cooperatives in the marketing of farm products, retailing and wholesaling, and credit unions and caisses populaires.

Some variations of the business model fit our conception of social economy businesses. The trend to merging business and social objectives, or creating a business with a social purpose, was inspired, in part, by Muhammad Yunus and the Grameen Bank and the related microfinance movement that he helped to create (Yunus, 2010). Both in Canada and internationally, modified business arrangements have been created such as the community interest company in the United Kingdom and the community contribution company (CCC) in British Columbia (BC). In BC this intent is clear (Small Business BC, 2015, p. 1): "The CCC is the first hybrid business structure of its kind in Canada, and allows entrepreneurs in BC to pursue social goals through their businesses while still generating a profit and providing investment opportunities to like-minded investors." These modified arrangements place restrictions on the use of profits in either a dividend distribution or sale.

Similarly, the MaRS Centre for Impact Investing (2016) in Toronto promotes certified B corporations, which it describes as "a new type of corporation which uses the power of business to solve social and environmental problems" (p. 1). Certification is done through B Lab, a US organization, and unlike the certification in British Columbia, it lacks any legal standing. It is simply a status symbol or signifier but, interestingly, one with which some businesses are pleased to be associated.

In summary, there are a large variety of organizations in the social economy, but all are guided by their social objectives. These social objectives differ, yet they share the following features:

1.   A social economy organization's social objectives can take many forms, but in general there should be a public benefit; put differently, the primary focus of the organization's assets, income, and human resources (paid and unpaid) is to meet social objectives.

2. Social economy organizations are self-governing and relatively independent from either government or the private sector in determining their
policies.

3. There is a constraint in distributing surplus income for individual gain,
excepting a rebate to members for patronage or use of services.

1.6   *Visualizing the Social Economy*

Rather than focusing on the social economy as a unique entity separate from
the private and public sectors, we view the three together as a mixed economy.
This can be represented in the Venn diagram in Figure 1. Although the components appear to be the same size in the diagram, in reality their sizes vary
across time and context (Hall, 2005; Martin, 1985) and also between countries
under different political and economic regimes (Salamon et al., 1999). Some
countries, Canada being one, have a very strong social economy with a range
of organizations offering services and innovation.

Social economy organizations perform many different functions in society
and have different forms of interactions with the private and public sectors. To
be in the social economy, it is important to remember that the organizations
must be guided by their social objectives. As noted, the social objectives are
not an add-on or afterthought to enhance public image: they are central to the
organization's *raison d'être*.

Looking specifically at the social economy in Figure 1, there are four subcomponents: (1) social economy businesses (SEBs), including social enterprises
that support a nonprofit parent organization; (2) community economic development (CED) organizations, which include social enterprises supported by
government programs; (3) public sector nonprofits; and (4) civil society organizations. The first three subcomponents—SEBs, CED organizations, and public
sector non-profits—are based on differing forms of overlap with the private
and public sectors and, therefore, could be considered as hybrid arrangements.
Civil society organizations have less overlap with the public and private sectors; however, civil society organizations interact with these other sectors in
important ways, and they represent the largest group of SEOs.

The Venn diagram, which has been used by other researchers in this field
(e.g., Billis, 2010; Bouchard, 2009; Pestoff, 1998; Quarter, Mook, & Armstrong,
2009, 2018), is useful because it signifies dynamic interaction. The social economy, albeit containing organizations with distinct characteristics, is an integral
and fluid part of society. Although the organizations in the social economy are
sometimes referred to as the "third sector," that label minimizes their importance to society. It is unimaginable to think of a modern, pluralistic society

SOCIAL ECONOMY

FIGURE 1   The social economy: an interactive approach
SOURCE: QUARTER, MOOK, & ARMSTRONG (2018), P. 16. REPRINTED WITH
PERMISSION OF THE PUBLISHER.

without the cultural, educational, professional, social, and business organizations that are central to the social economy. This is even more so since the
advent of the Internet, which has vastly enlarged what counts as a community
and has facilitated rapid, global communication. Therefore, we refer to our
framework as an *interactive approach*.

The four components of the social economy presented in the Venn diagram
in Figure 1 not only have differing forms of interaction with the private and public sectors, but also within themselves. Within civil society, for example, sharp
debates surround issues such as carbon taxes, abortion, and the rights of same-
sex couples, sparking conflicting views among participating organizations.
Environmental groups—some small organizations using volunteers and others well-endowed international organizations—criticize government and
corporate policies, although some other associations may defend them. The
organizations that are the focal point of these debates receive funding from different interest groups in society, some wanting the current policies to remain
in place and others wanting fundamental changes.

The Venn diagram can also help to understand that the interactions among the components of the social economy and their relationship to the other sectors are not static and are constantly changing. For example, with the pressure from business interests to reduce taxes and the size of government, organizations in the social economy have had to adapt themselves to a funding regime that emphasizes efficiency and to be more like private sector businesses. Many nonprofit organizations are employing more business-like models, though not without concern that adopting business practices might compromise social commitments, a practice that is referred to as *mission drift* (Eikenberry & Kluver, 2004; Hall, 1992). The wealthy are also engaging in forms of charitable practice that have more of a business bent, for example, venture philanthropy with its increased emphasis on strategic investment and measuring outcomes.

Similarly, there is pressure from civil society on for-profit corporations to act in more socially responsible ways and to take into consideration the social costs of environmental pollution, hazardous workplaces, unhealthy foods, wasteful packaging, and so on. Due to competitive pressures and enlightened leadership, some corporations are attempting to integrate within a profit model practices that reflect greater social responsibility. Moreover, new "hybrid" organizations (Billis, 2010; Rifkin, 2014) are being created to combine business expertise with social goals. A new breed of entrepreneur called a *social entrepreneur* is seeking to design businesses so that they blend clearly defined social objectives from their inception (Drayton & Budinich, 2010; Martin & Osberg, 2015; Prahalad & Hammond, 2002). In an age of heightened competition and globalization, we can likely expect more, not less, fluidity at the boundaries of the public, private, and social economy sectors.

1.7 Introducing the Components of the Social Economy
The social economy contains many different types of organizations that are represented within the four components of the Venn diagram: (1) social economy businesses (SEBS); (2) community economic development (CED) organizations, including social enterprises supported by government programs and foundations; (3) public sector nonprofits; and (4) civil society organizations. These four components reveal crucial ways in which organizations differ from each other in purpose, structure, financing, and governance.

It is important to remember that the Venn diagram helps to visualize how different types of organizations in the social economy may be situated. It may be difficult to place certain organizations neatly into one component or another; however, it is a valuable tool to differentiate social organizations in terms of their ownership, governance, and funding characteristics.

1.7.1   Social Economy Businesses

In the Venn diagram, SEBs are in the overlap between the social economy and the private sector. SEBs are a hybrid arrangement with one foot in the private sector and another in the social economy. Like private sector businesses in general, SEBs earn either all or a predominant portion of their revenues from the marketplace, but they place a strong emphasis on their social objectives rather than simply on profit and shareholder value, as is the usual business imperative.

Many social economy businesses are cooperatives that earn their revenues from the market, for example, credit unions, farm marketing and other marketing cooperatives, and consumer cooperatives such as goods retailing or grocery cooperatives. Other examples include nonprofit organizations such as the Canadian Automobile Association (CAA), Blue Cross, farmers' markets, recreational organizations such as the YMCA, social enterprises that generate revenues for a nonprofit parent organization, and Aboriginal businesses that support a sponsoring community. All of these are SEBs, and while they all operate in the market and compete with conventional businesses, they all strive to meet social objectives, including meeting the needs of their members.

1.7.2   Community Economic Development Organizations

Community economic development organizations are a hybrid arrangement portrayed in the Venn diagram as being in the overlap between the social economy and the private and public sectors. The principal characteristic of CED organizations is that they combine public and private resources to build or strengthen community assets for social benefit. Like other organizations in the social economy, CED organizations prioritize their social objectives. In this case, they contribute to the development of their local communities, and like SEBs, CED organizations sell their services in the market. But unlike SEBs, CED organizations rely on external support from government programs and foundations. This dependence of the CED organization on external support occurs for differing reasons, including the following: its location is in an impoverished part of the country; the group it represents suffers social disadvantages (such as being a minority status with a history of oppression); it represents recent immigrants in need of assistance; or it employs people with serious disabilities (psychiatric, intellectual, and/or physical) who rely on disability pensions and other support. Examples of CED organizations are: community development corporations, community benefits agreement coalitions, performing arts organizations, online CED organizations and supported social enterprises for marginalized social groups, both training and employment organizations.

1.7.3   Public Sector Nonprofit Organizations

Organizations shown in the overlap between the social economy and the public sector are labelled as *public sector nonprofits* because they have one foot in the social economy and one foot in the public sector. These hybrid organizations are self-governing with their own board of directors and incorporation. They receive substantial funding through government programs and are guided to varying degrees by government policies. Typically, public sector nonprofits are in service areas such as higher education, health care, nonprofit housing, and child care. Some are cooperatives.

Public sector nonprofit organizations can interact with government in differing ways, with some being very closely aligned (as a service delivery extension of government) and others having greater independence. Public sector nonprofits may also earn revenues from the sale of their services, but they are providing a public service and receive at least some guidance from government policy.

Some argue that the arrangement between public sector nonprofits and government is a productive partnership with each party undertaking what it does best: government provides a substantial portion of the funding and some policy direction, and the nonprofits themselves, which are more in touch with local communities, determine how to best offer the service (Salamon, 1987, 1995; Salamon & Anheier, 1997). Others view the relationship more critically and suggest that government is intruding on the management of nonprofits (Akingbola, 2004; Smith & Lipsky, 1993). In part, these concerns arise because governments, in response to criticism, have moved away from grants and core funding to contracts that are of a shorter term with more onerous reporting than has existed in the past. Both viewpoints have merit. Although the partnership between government and public sector nonprofits appears to be productive, more stringent funding arrangements are challenging for many public sector nonprofits. This has forced them to consider funding alternatives other than government.

1.7.4   Civil Society Organizations

Civil society organizations are neither public nor private sector organizations but interact with these sectors because their members may work there, their donors may come from those sectors, or they may relate to those sectors through their services. Civil society organizations include the following four broad groupings: (1) nonprofit mutual associations relating primarily to the economy, such as unions, professional associations, and consumer groups; (2) nonprofit mutual associations focusing on social needs, such as religious groups, associations of race and ethnicity, and self-help groups that serve a defined membership having a mutual or shared interest that they seek to satisfy through the organization; (3) member-based associations that serve the public, either at large or specific groups of people in need, such as political parties and other sociopolitical advocacy associations (e.g., environmental groups or feminist associations) and service clubs (e.g., the Lions, the Shriners, and the Elks); and (4) different forms of foundations and fundraising mechanisms serving the public, including the United Way, community foundations (e.g., the Community Foundation of Newfoundland and Labrador and the Winnipeg Foundation), private and public foundations (e.g., the J. W. McConnell Family Foundation and the Canada West Foundation), and newer approaches, such as crowdfunding.

Civil society organizations tend to associate with each other around common purposes. Often there is an apex or umbrella organization that becomes the voice of member organizations with a common bond of association, for example, the Canadian Environmental Network (CEN) serves that function for environmental organizations across Canada, the Canadian Labour Congress (CLC) for unions, and the Canadian Ethnocultural Council (CEC) for break ethno-/ cultural groups. The list is extensive. One organization's bonds of association can extend into many networks, or put differently, the organization may find many commonalities with many other organizations in our highly networked society. A religious organization may also be an ethnocultural organization and be part of networks related to reducing poverty (e.g., Kairos Canada). Organizations do not necessarily, however, associate with each other because they are part of a common sector called the social economy or the nonprofit or the voluntary sector.

1.8   *Bringing It All Together: Why the Social Economy?*

The many types of organizations within the social economy differ from each other, while sharing the common denominator of being guided by their social objectives. Social economy organizations are diverse and multifunctional. Our classification system underlines that certain social economy organizations have common functions that transcend their incorporation; for example, they earn their income from selling their services in the market, much like a business. Social economy organizations can be commercial nonprofits or cooperatives with shares.

Our classification system is imperfect, especially since our world is in such rapid flux, and organizational forms are changing before our eyes (North, 2005). As might be surmised from our analysis, we are, however, using two primary dimensions—the source of the organization's funding and the organization's orientation, or the characteristics of the groups being served.

For example, social economy businesses, as noted, earn their revenues from the market, much like other businesses in that regard, but some SEBs serve the public at large (anyone who wants to purchase their services); other SEBs serve a membership, as is the case for some cooperatives and nonprofit mutual associations, the membership being a particular public.

Community economic development organizations, too, are oriented to a market for a portion of their revenues, but they typically receive revenues from other sources, such as government programs, foundations, and donors, and they benefit from volunteer contributions. Many CED organizations are social enterprises serving marginalized social groups. CED organizations may have a membership, but in all cases, their orientation is to a local community.

Public sector nonprofit organizations obtain a substantial portion of their revenues from government agencies supplemented by grants from foundations, donors, and some sale of services. As their name implies, public sector nonprofits offer a service to the public, in particular, a specific public, such as people in need of housing and/or child care, and often with low incomes.

Civil society organizations, the most diverse of our classifications, usually derive their revenues from many sources, for example, donations, membership fees, foundations, sale of services, and government grants and contracts. Many civil society SEOs are oriented to serving their membership: unions, professional associations, religious organizations, social clubs, and so on. Other civil society SEOs are oriented to serving the public, for example, social movement groups, public service organizations, and foundations.

As noted, an important feature of our framework is the emphasis on the interaction of the sectors. The social economy is not a standalone entity but a vital part of a mixed economy. Salamon (1987, 1995) discusses the interaction between nonprofit organizations and government and refers to it as a partnership. Others (Akingbola, 2004; Smith & Lipsky, 1993) are more critical and view it not as a partnership, but as a form of government domination. Market failure theorists (Ben-Ner, 1986; Hansmann, 1980; Weisbrod, 1975, 1977) explain how nonprofit organizations interact with the market, based on their argument that nonprofits assume roles in which business markets fail.

Like these other scholars, our conceptual framework emphasizes interaction but differing forms of interaction—not just one. The interaction for social economy businesses differs from that of public sector nonprofits or civil society organizations. In fact, even though we discuss many different forms of interaction, we feel that we are just scratching the surface.

2   The Scope and Size of the Social Economy Sector

Canada has a vast social economy, but there is no single source of data that
brings together its scope and size. However, we can get a sense of it by looking at its different components: formal and informal nonprofit organizations,
cooperatives, and social enterprises.

2.1   *Nonprofit Organizations*[1]
The first (and so far only) comprehensive national study of Canadian formal
nonprofit and voluntary organizations, the National Survey of Nonprofit and
Voluntary Organizations (NSNVO), was conducted in 2003 by Statistics Canada
in conjunction with Imagine Canada. Although dated, it provides an overall
look at these organizations.
    To be included in the survey, organizations had to meet the following
criteria:
– non-governmental (i.e., are institutionally separate from governments)
– nonprofit distributing (i.e., do not return any profits generated to their owners or directors)
– self-governing (i.e., are independent and able to regulate their own activities)
– voluntary (i.e., benefit to some degree from voluntary contributions of time
   or money)
– formally incorporated or registered under specific legislation with provincial, territorial, or federal governments. (Hall, de Wit et al., 2005, p. 8)
In terms of a formal nonprofit sector following these criteria, Canada is second
in size globally after the Netherlands (Hall, Barr, et al., 2005).[2] The study found
that there were about 161,000 incorporated nonprofit organizations in Canada,
on average (at that time) 29 years old, and about half were charities (Hall, de
Wit, et al., 2005). This is forecasted to be now over 170,000 (Imagine Canada,
2014). There are many more informal groups and organizations such as grassroots associations (Smith, 1997a, 1997b). Although there is no estimate of the
number of such groups for Canada, other research estimated that formal nonprofits made up only about 12–17% of all nonprofits (Smith, 2006).
    Just over 12% of Canada's charities are private or public foundations (about
10,800 out of 86,400 in February 2018). Private foundations, in which 50% or

---

1   The nonprofit sector in Canada is often discussed in terms of the *overall* nonprofit sector and
    the *core* nonprofit sector. The *overall* nonprofit sector includes institutions such as hospitals,
    residential care facilities, universities and colleges. These organizations are typically large
    and regulated by government. They are also referred to as QUANGOS—quasi-autonomous
    non-governmental organizations. The *core* nonprofit sector excludes these organizations.
2   The US nonprofit sector is ranked number 5 on this list.

more of their governing officials operate at non-arm's length with each other, account for 53% of all foundations. This is up almost 7% from three years prior. The number of public foundations on the other hand decreased by about 2% in this same time period (Philanthropic Foundations Canada, 2018).

Whereas in the US foundations tend to play a welfare-replacement role to address areas where the state is inactive, in Canada they play more of a complementary role (Elson et al., 2018). They are particularly active in funding the areas of education and research, health, and social services.

There is a growing trend of foundations working together in funder collectives as a form of strategic philanthropy facilitated by key networks such as the Community Foundations of Canada (CFC), Philanthropic Foundations Canada (PFC), and Canadian Environmental Grantmakers Network (CEGN) (Glass & Pole, 2017). Foundations are also coming together to understand, educate, and build new relationships with Canada's Indigenous peoples (Elson et al., 2018). Many, along with educational institutions and the nonprofit sector in general have signed onto a *Declaration of Action* toward the shared goal of reconciliation and are working collaboratively in this regard (The Circle, 2018).

The most prevalent nonprofit organizations are sports and recreation organizations (21%), followed by religion (19%), social services (12%), grant-making, fundraising and voluntarism promotion (10%), and arts and culture (9%) (Hall, de Wit, et al., 2005) (see Table 1). There is some variation regionally, but generally religion accounts for the highest percentage of all organizations in the majority of provinces, with sports and recreation highest in Alberta, Quebec, and the Territories (Hall, de Wit, et al., 2005). When you look at areas of activity for charities only, religion is first (32%), followed by social services (15%), and grant-making, fundraising, and voluntarism promotion (14%).

Looking at the size of the sector in terms of revenues, hospitals, universities, and colleges account for one-third, even though they make up only 1.2% of all nonprofits. The main sources of revenue are government funding (49%), earned income from non-governmental sources (35%), and gifts and donations (13%) (Hall, de Wit, et al., 2005). This varies according to area of activity. For instance, hospitals received over 80% of their funding from government sources.

As mentioned previously, there are also many unincorporated nonprofits, including farmers' markets, hobby groups, community associations, union locals, and advocacy groups. These are generally very small; however, many still operate with a formal structure with executives and bylaws. Members are attracted to these organizations because of their social mission, and are a core resource through volunteering their time. Other key resources for these organizations include membership fees and grants. Generally, these groups do not

TABLE 1   Distribution of nonprofit and voluntary organizations by area of activity

Primary Activity Area	% of all Organizations	% of all Charities	% of all Revenues	% of all Volunteer Hours	% of all Paid Staff
Sports and recreation	20.9	10.1	5.4	22.8	6.4
Religion	19.0	32.1	6.1*	12.2	5.4*
Social services	11.8	15.3	10.0	20.4*	14.6
Grant-making, fundraising, and voluntarism promotion	9.9	14.0	7.4	6.8	1.4
Arts and culture	8.5	8.3	3.1	8.5	3.6
Development and housing	7.6	3.1	5.9	1.4	9.0*
Business and professional associations and unions	5.3	0.7	9.7	2.8	7.4*
Education and research	5.1	5.1	5.9	6.7*	5.0
Health	3.3	4.7	8.2	5.5	9.5
Environment	2.7	2.0	1.0	1.2	0.7
Law, advocacy, and politics	2.3	1.4	1.3	3.5*	0.8
Organizations not elsewhere classified	2.1	1.2	1.9	3.4*	1.7
International	0.6	0.9	1.1	2.3	0.3
Hospitals	0.5	0.8	21.9	1.9	23.8
Universities and colleges	0.3	0.4	11.1	0.6	10.5

*   Use with caution.
SOURCE: HALL, DE WIT, ET AL. (2005), COMPILED FROM PP. 23, 33, 38 WITH % OF CHARITIES CALCULATED BY AUTHORS BASED ON PP. 14, 15.

have an interest in incorporation because the additional resources needed and the added burden of reporting outweigh any perceived benefits of doing so (Akingbola, 2013).

In terms of governance, one study of larger, older health and welfare nonprofits found that about 44% of board members are women; however, representation of visible minorities and different ethnic groups is low (Bradshaw & Fredette, 2012). Organizational size and size of the board were statistically significant factors in determining diversity, with larger organizations and larger boards tending to be more diverse. There was no relationship however to the age of the organization. A national study from decades earlier found similar results in terms of gender (Bradshaw, Murray, & Wolpin, 1996).

2.2 Cooperatives

The social economy is also home to a large number of financial and non-financial cooperatives, a form of mutual association that sometimes is with share capital, sometimes without share capital, or a nonprofit. A cooperative is defined by the International Cooperative Alliance as "an autonomous association of persons united voluntarily to meet their common economic, social, and cultural needs and aspirations through a jointly owned and democratically-controlled enterprise" (ICA, 2018, p. 1). They are democratically managed according to the "one member, one vote" rule, and many follow an aspirational set of values and principles (ICA, 2018, p. 1):

Cooperative values
Cooperatives are based on the values of self-help, self-responsibility, democracy, equality, equity and solidarity. In the tradition of their founders, cooperative members believe in the ethical values of honesty, openness, social responsibility and caring for others.

Cooperative Principles
The cooperative principles are guidelines by which cooperatives put their values into practice:
1. Voluntary and Open Membership
2. Democratic Member Control
3. Member Economic Participation
4. Autonomy and Independence
5. Education, Training, and Information
6. Cooperation among Cooperatives
7. Concern for Community

There are many reasons that an organization might be formed as a cooperative including "unavailability or instability of work; products and services that are overpriced; improved market access for producers through co-operation; and better working conditions through collective enterprises" (Co-op Canada, 2018, p. 1). Cooperatives also perform multiple roles in market economies: "internalize market externalities, to serve as laboratories for social innovation, to espouse social entrepreneurship, to promote ethical business practices, and to aid in development" (Novkovic, 2008, p. 2168). Joining together in a cooperative provides many socioeconomic benefits for members. Members of producer cooperatives can protect themselves from unstable markets and risk by pooling together and providing storage facilities. Worker cooperatives provide protection from job loss with organization survival rates much higher than conventional businesses. One reason for this may be high member engagement (Vieta et al., 2016). Housing cooperatives may provide low-income housing, while credit unions provide lower-cost services for their members (Novkovic & Gordon Nembhard, 2017).

Non-financial cooperatives are created under either the *Canada Cooperatives Act* if they operate and have an office in at least two provinces/territories, or otherwise under a provincial/territorial Cooperatives Act. Although organizations and groups can operate informally on a cooperative basis, they cannot use the work "co-op" or "cooperative" in their name unless they are formally incorporated. There is also separate incorporation of credit unions (financial cooperatives) at the provincial or federal level, for instance the *Credit Unions and Caisses Populaires Act* in Ontario.

Credit unions have a long tradition of innovation in Canada as they respond to the needs of their members. Some of those innovations include: "the first financial institution to lend to women in their own names (in the 1960s), first to offer daily interest savings, first full service ATMS, first fully functional online banking, first debit card service, and first cheque imaging service" (CCUA, 2016, p. 1). Credit unions as compared to banks are more likely to be found in areas of material deprivation, such as areas of low income, high unemployment, and a higher proportion of those receiving government transfer payments (Maiorano, Mook, & Quarter, 2016).

As of the end of 2017, there were 567 credit unions and caisses populaires in 2,787 locations across the country, serving over 10.25 million members. Total assets of these institutions amount to $391 billion, with $309 billion in savings and $329 billion in loans (CCUA, 2018b). When compared to population size, there is a greater proportion of credit unions in rural and small-town areas than cities (30.7% of population with 53.5% of credit unions) (Mook, Hann, & Quarter, 2012).

There are also a variety of non-financial cooperatives in Canada including consumer co-ops (69%), producer co-ops (16%), multi-stakeholder co-ops (9%), and worker co-ops (5%). They can be found in housing, agriculture, retail, health care and social services, manufacturing, high-speed broadband, and clean energy (Industry Canada, 2018). Industry Canada estimates there are just over 8,000 non-financial co-ops in Canada (Industry Canada, 2018).

There is some regional variation in the prevalence of co-ops across Canada. Most of the business activity of agriculture, forestry, fishing and hunting co-ops, construction and manufacturing co-ops, transportation and warehousing co-ops, professional, scientific and technical services, and educational service co-ops, and health care and social assistance co-ops are found in Quebec. Alberta generates most of the utilities co-op business volume, as well as business from finance and insurance co-ops. Wholesale and retail trade are highest in Saskatchewan. Real estate and leasing co-ops are highest in Ontario. Waste management and remediation service co-ops have the highest business volume in Quebec, but Nova Scotia is close behind (Industry Canada, 2018).

Ontario has a healthy cooperative sector, second only to Quebec. Historically, its strength was in the agriculture sector, but today the largest number of co-ops (45%) are in the housing sector and the rest are quite diverse. However, it has not yet been able to garner dedicated cooperative support from its government in the form of a broad sectoral and cooperative support programs due in part to a volatile political environment and high turnover in government administrators (Heneberry & Laforest, 2011).

As the co-op movement expanded in Quebec over the last few decades, it declined in other areas of Canada. Membership, assets, and revenues in Saskatchewan non-financial cooperatives dropped by 8%, 12% and 45% respectively from 1995 to 2005, while it doubled, quadrupled, and doubled respectively in Quebec (Diamantopoulos, 2011). The decrease in Saskatchewan has been explained by the collapse of middle farmers due to neo-liberal reforms and deregulation, the dismantlement of farm subsidies, and the implementation of free trade agreements. In Quebec, on the other hand, persistently high unemployment rates led to public and cooperative action to create jobs with pressure from the women's movement and unions (Arsenault, 2018; Diamantopoulos, 2011). A number of sector–state partnerships were formed, and a network coordinated by the Regional Development Cooperative (CDRQ) was launched throughout the province providing support and resources for cooperative development. New areas of employment such as worker cooperatives, worker–shareholder cooperatives, and solidarity cooperatives emerged (Diamantopoulos, 2011).

In Atlantic Canada, the Antigonish Movement that started in the 1920s as a response to economic hardships in the region established cooperatives and credit unions so that people could take control of their own destinies (Lionais, 2015). Through education, mass public meetings, and small study clubs, cooperatives were organized. At the height of the movement, over 240 cooperatives were created across multiple sectors including fisheries, agriculture, finance, housing, and retail. These enterprises continued to flourish across the province until the 1960s, when second-generation leadership "arguably, lost sight of the transformative vision of the movement" and cooperative development declined (Lionais, 2015, p. 27). There are however several regions in Atlantic Canada where the cooperative movement is still strong, for example the Evangeline Region of Prince Edward Island and the Acadian communities of Cheticamp in Nova Scotia (Lionais, 2015).

Although cooperatives are reputed to be more egalitarian than other types of organizations, a gender analysis of cooperative boards finds that only 27% of board members are women while noting this is still twice as high as corporate boards where less than 14% are women. Men are five times as likely to hold the chair position on co-op boards (CCA/BGI, 2009). There are no national studies looking at the intersectionality of gender and race in cooperative leadership, however this is an area that is gaining attention (Sengupta, 2015).

According to Industry Canada's latest survey (66% response rate), almost half (49%) the reporting non-financial cooperatives in Canada operate without paid staff. While the number of these co-ops is high, they account for only 2% of co-op revenues and 12% of co-op assets. At the other end of the scale, there are about 320 co-ops with more than 500 employees, and these co-ops account for 59% of co-op revenues and 47% of co-op assets (Industry Canada, 2018).

2.3   *Social Enterprises*

Social enterprises are businesses that have social objectives but operate in the market. Charities in Canada who operate social enterprises do so mostly through subsidiary organizations as the Income Tax Act prohibits them from carrying on an unrelated business. Efforts are being made to lobby to loosen this restriction, which may in turn spur an increase in social enterprises in the future (Larre, 2016).

A conceptual study of social enterprises in Canada as part of the International Comparative Social Enterprise Models (ICSEM) project classified five types of social enterprises: (1) cooperatives; (2) nonprofit organizations; (3) community development/interest organizations; (4) indigenous businesses; and (5) businesses with a social mission. The last type includes Community Interest Companies (CIC) or Community Contribution Companies (CCC) (McMurtry & Brouard, 2015).

The impetus for starting social enterprises varies across regions. In Atlantic Canada, poverty and unemployment due to a chronically weak economy has spurred different development over time. In the 1970s and 1980s, a small number of community-controlled business corporations were started through the leadership of Greg MacLeod, a community activist and professor at Cape Breton University, rooted in community development. Today, social enterprises in this region have been initiated through the influx of resources from wealthy investors rather than driven by community; however, the goal is still to revive local economies (Lionais, 2015). Several provincial policies provide incentives for this investment, including the Community Economic Development Investment Fund and legislation to create a new organizational form called the community interest company (CIC).

In Ontario, the political context in the 1980s of cost-cutting and self-sufficiency in public service, as well as the North American Free Trade Agreement (NAFTA), influenced a focus on social enterprise as a response to the impact of these changes (Brouard, McMurtry, & Vieta, 2015). There was also a strong focus on entrepreneurship and innovation. The Ontario government created an Office of Social Enterprise in 2012, and now has a social enterprise strategy for the province with the goal of "making Ontario the best place in North America to start, grow and invest in social enterprises" (SEOntario, 2018, p. 1).

In Western Canada, the social enterprise landscape was driven by community leaders through the creation of Enterprising Non-Profits in British Columbia, the Social Enterprise Fund in Alberta, and the Canadian CED Network in Manitoba (Elson et al., 2015). Enterprising Non-Profits arose out of a pilot project of the Vancity Community Foundation along with the Vancouver Foundation and the United Way of Lower Mainland. The Social Enterprise Fund was a product of the Edmonton Community Foundation and the City of Edmonton. The Canadian CED Network in Manitoba is a network of associations concerned with community economy development and, as such, organized a social enterprise working group in 2013 to coordinate a social enterprise ecosystem. They co-created a social enterprise strategy with the provincial government in 2015 focusing on six areas: "enhancing entrepreneurial skills; ensuring access to capital and investment; expanding market opportunities; promoting and demonstrating the value of social enterprise; improving regulatory frameworks; and creating networks and community engagement" (Elson et al., 2015, p. 92).

In Indigenous communities, social enterprise development is influenced by geography, economic factors, and a history of colonization (Sengupta, Vieta, & McMurtry, 2015). Social enterprises started by Indigenous communities are qualitatively different from other social enterprises, holistically combining economic, social, environmental, and cultural goals. These socio-economic goals include: "(i) greater control of activities on their traditional lands, (ii) self-determination and an end to dependency through economic self-sufficiency, (iii) the preservation and strengthening of traditional values and their application in economic development and business activities, and of course (iv) improved socioeconomic circumstance for individuals, families, and communities through social entrepreneurship" (Anderson, Dana, & Dana, 2006, p. 47).

As noted by Bouchard, Cruz Filho, and Zerdani (2015), the term "social enterprise" is not commonly used in Quebec. However, Quebec does recognize the concept of social economy enterprises or collective enterprises. These are autonomous and independent enterprises operated by a cooperative, mutual society, or association, that sell or exchange goods and services, with democratic governance and limited or prohibited profit distribution.

McMurtry and Brouard (2015) find that the emergence of social enterprise in English-speaking Canada has been influenced by five distinct traditions. First is the USA and its focus on entrepreneurship and self-sufficiency. Next is the influence of the United Kingdom social enterprise movement which is more socially focused with elements of community ownership and social care. Third is the contribution of continental Europe's understanding of social enterprise based on democratic practice and community control. Fourth are indigenous communities' understandings of social enterprise community economic development. Finally, are the experiences of Canada's diverse immigrant communities prior to arriving in Canada, and also from difficulties faced once they arrived.[3]

In 2014 and 2015, a series of ten regional surveys of social enterprises across Canada (except Quebec) provided a first look at their location, purpose, and operations. Social enterprises in these surveys were defined as, "a business venture owned or operated by a nonprofit organization that sells goods or provides services in the market for the purpose of creating a blended return on investment, both financial and social/environmental/cultural" (Elson, Hall, & Wamucii, 2016, p. 8). About three-quarters of the reporting social enterprises operate as nonprofits, and just over 20% operate as cooperatives. Over half (56%) are registered charities. About two-thirds of the social enterprises reported not having a parent organization, and of those with a parent organization, about two-thirds received support from them in the form of personnel. The results show most social enterprises have been operating for at least twenty years (54%). In terms of business sectors, more than half of social enterprises can be found selling goods and providing services in multiple areas. About 40% could be found in the accommodation, food, and tourism sector, 36% in professional services, and 31% in arts, culture, and communications.

The surveys identified three mutually exclusive purposes of social enterprises: first, to generate income for a parent nonprofit organization (12%); second, to fulfill a social, cultural, or environmental mandate (60%); and third,

---

3   For an overview of the historical antecedents of the social economy and social enterprise tradition in Quebec, see Brouard, Cruz Filho, and Zerdani (2015).

multiple purposes that include providing employment and training for workforce integration (28%) (Elson, Hall, & Wamucii, 2016, p. 8).

In terms of revenues, about 70% of reported income was derived from the sale of goods and services. About three-quarters of the social enterprises received grants or contributions from other sources. The most prevalent sources were grants from provincial governments (almost half received this type of funding) and contributions from private individuals (42%). These grants were used primarily for operations (71%). About three-quarters broke even, and 40% broke even without grants. Most did not take out loans (74%), and those that did were just as likely to go to a bank (8%) as a credit union (7%). The purposes of those loans were primarily for capital and for operations (Elson, Hall, & Wamucii, 2016, p. 8).

An analysis of three of these regional surveys (Ontario, British Columbia, and Alberta) looked specifically at non-earned income, that is, grants and donations, and found that social enterprises oriented towards poverty alleviation and in lower-income neighborhoods received less non-earned income than other types of social enterprise (Liston-Heyes et al., 2017). Culture and arts-oriented social enterprises were more likely to secure grants and donations. Non-earned income was easier to access if the social enterprise was located in a higher-income neighborhood and less likely to be secured if the social enterprise operated at only a local level as they were typically smaller and with less capacity to secure grants. Age of the social enterprise also played a factor with younger organizations more likely to have non-earned income. Overall, these particular data show that donor preferences, neighborhood wealth and geographical visibility all influenced the level of non-earned income for these organizations (Liston-Heyes et al., 2017).

On average as a group, social enterprises employed ten full-time employees, seven part-time employees and four seasonal employees. About 15% had no paid staff, and about 60% had under ten full-time employees. About 43% had an employment purpose of addressing poverty by targeting individuals with employment barriers. Almost one-third (29%) train, employ, or provide services to Aboriginal or Indigenous people (Elson, Hall, & Wamucii, 2016).

3 Research on Voluntaristic Behaviors Enabling the Social Economy

The extent of giving, volunteering, and participating of Canadians is more consistently tracked, starting with the National Survey of Giving, Volunteering, and Participating in 1997. The latest is the 2013 General Social Survey Giving, Volunteering, and Participating survey (2013 GSS GVP). There were different instrument designs used over the years, so the later results are not strictly comparable to the earlier ones.

3.1   *Giving*

Based on the 2013 GSS GVP survey, over 80% of Canadians aged fifteen and older make financial donations to charities or other nonprofit organizations. Two-thirds of donations are made by 10% of donors; 84% of all donations are made by 25% of donors (Turcotte, 2015a, 2015c). In 2013, the total of this giving was estimated as $12.8 billion, an average of $531 per year per donor (Turcotte, 2015a). The amount of giving increases with the age of donor, with donors aged seventy-five and older averaging $726 per donor. Men tend to give more on average ($580) than women ($484), and women tend to give more to religious organizations while men give more to non-religious organizations.

There is some regional variation as to average annual donations, with a high of an average of $863 per donor in Alberta and a low of $264 per donor in Quebec (Turcotte, 2015a). However, demographic and socioeconomic factors play a role here, in particular religiosity and household income. If you take into account all respondents to the GSS GVP (not just the givers), these amounts are $734 for Alberta and $213 for Quebec (Devlin & Zhao, 2017). Taking into consideration these factors, the financial donations of Quebeckers move from lowest in the group to seventh place out of ten, and for donations to religious organizations in particular, from last to fourth place (Devlin & Zhao, 2017). About 60% of all donations go to secular organizations overall (Table 2).

About 40% of giving is to religious organizations, half of this coming from donors aged fifty-five and over. For non-religious organizations, health sector and social services organizations received 25% of donations (Turcotte, 2015b). The most common reasons indicated by Canadian who gave money were "they felt compassion towards people in need" (91%) and "to help a cause in which they personally believed" (88%) (Turcotte, 2015b, p. 14). About half (47%) of donors do not research new organizations to which they donate (Turcotte, 2015b). Of those who do research new organizations, they are most likely to get that information by contacting the organization or from its website. Only one-fifth (18%) of donors are aware of watchdog organizations that monitor charities.

Less than half (48%) of Canadians who made donations to charitable organizations in 2013 planned on taking a tax credit for those donations, even though they could receive about half the value of the donation back (Turcotte, 2015b). This percentage increases as the amount of donations increased, with 78% of those donating $500 or more planning to take the tax credit.

Canadians also donate goods and food at a high rate. In 2013, 60% of Canadians donated food to a charitable organization, and 76% donated

TABLE 2 Average donations by province, n = 14,699

	Average total donations per respondent	Average to religious organizations	Average to secular organizations	% going to religious organizations	% going to secular organizations
Canada	$437	$179	$258	41%	59%
British Columbia	$549	$232	$318	42%	58%
Alberta	$734	$277	$456	38%	62%
Saskatchewan	$576	$258	$318	45%	55%
Manitoba	$588	$266	$322	45%	55%
Ontario	$443	$186	$257	42%	58%
Quebec	$213	$73	$140	34%	66%
Nova Scotia	$332	$156	$176	47%	53%
New Brunswick	$287	$147	$140	51%	49%
Newfoundland & Labrador	$306	$154	$152	50%	50%
Prince Edward Island	$416	$209	$207	50%	50%

SOURCE: DEVLIN & ZHAO (2017). P. 25; PERCENTAGES CALCULATED BY AUTHORS.

clothing, toys, or household items (Turcotte, 2015b). Women give food (66%) and material goods (82%) at a higher rate than men. Individuals of thirty-five years and older give at a higher rate than those under thirty-five (Turcotte, 2015b).

3.2   Formal Volunteering

Six out of every ten Canadians aged fifteen or older have volunteered at some point in their lives. In 2013, 12.7 million volunteers reported contributing almost 2 billion hours of work, which is the equivalent of one million full-time jobs. Individually, this works out to an average of 154 hours during the year (Sinha, 2015; Turcotte, 2015a).[4] If you put a financial value on these hours using the average hourly rate in the nonprofit sector of $24.90, this amounts to $48.7 billion—over 1.8 times that of the GDP contributed by the nonprofit

---

4   The preamble to identify volunteers was, "Now, I'd like to ask you some questions about any activities that you did without pay on behalf of a group or an organization in the past 12 months. This includes any unpaid help you provided to schools, religious organizations, sports or community associations."

sector not including volunteers. The contribution of volunteers is estimated to contribute about 2.6% to Canada's GDP (Conference Board of Canada, 2018).

Looking at age groups, teenagers volunteer at the highest rate with two-thirds (66%) of those between the ages of fifteen and nineteen volunteering during the past year. One-fifth of teenage volunteers report being required to volunteer for school or some other reason (Sinha, 2015). Students in college are also encouraged to volunteer. In a study of college students aged twenty to twenty-four in five countries—Australia, Canada, New Zealand, the United Kingdom, and the US—students in Canada volunteered at the highest rate (80%) (Smith et al., 2010).

Volunteer rates in Canada generally decrease with age, with the exception of the age group of thirty-five to forty-four, which increases compared to the twenty to thirty-four age group. This increase is attributed to volunteering as part of a parental role, for instance, in schools and after-school programs. In this age category, significantly more women (52%) than men (44%) volunteer, the only age category where volunteer rates differed between women and men. Seniors have the lowest volunteer rates (38% for ages sixty-five to seventy-four, and 27% for those seventy-five and over). Over 40% of senior non-volunteers cite health reasons for not volunteering (Sinha, 2015).

In terms of socioeconomic status, those most likely to volunteer have a higher household income, higher educational attainment, and are currently in the labor force. Although those with a higher household income are more likely to volunteer, they contributed the fewest number of hours (130 hours per year) as compared to the lowest-income volunteers (182 hours per year). Immigrants to Canada who volunteer contribute the same average number of hours as Canadian-born volunteers; however, the volunteer rate is lower (38% versus 45%) (Sinha, 2015).

The most common pattern of volunteering according to the survey is on a weekly basis with 30% of volunteers giving their time this way. Twenty-five percent volunteer on a monthly basis, 7% on a daily basis, and the remaining 37% on an episodic basis of one to four times a year.

Over half of the volunteer hours (53%) are contributed by 10% of volunteers, who average 372 hours or more per year (and often referred to as dedicated volunteers). The top 25% of all volunteers contribute over three-quarters (77%) of all the hours over the year (Sinha, 2015).

Most volunteering occurs in the social services, with sports and recreation and religion following in terms of the percentage of all volunteer hours. The top volunteer activity is organizing events, followed by teaching or mentoring, sitting on a committee or board, office work or bookkeeping, and fundraising. Activities differ by gender, with women reporting more often that they were involved in fundraising, organizing events, and providing health care, and men more likely to coach and provide services related to maintenance or repair (Sinha, 2015).

Both Canadian and foreign-born volunteers play an important role in the settlement of newcomers to Canada. These volunteers help new immigrants prepare for job searches, learn about Canadian culture, expand social networks, and access community resources and services (Behnia, 2012). Studies find that "compared to other immigrants and refugees, immigrants and refugees who are matched with volunteers obtain employment sooner, perform better in language acquisition, receive less government financial assistance, have more friends, and are more optimistic about their future" (Behnia, 2012, p. 7).

As with giving, there is some regional variation in volunteering patterns. Compared to the national average volunteer rate of 44%, individuals in Quebec volunteer at a rate of 32% while those in Saskatchewan volunteer at a rate of 56% (Turcotte, 2015a).

Many businesses in Canada provide formal support for their employees to volunteer, and 55% of volunteers report participating in employer-supported volunteering. This includes use of facilities or equipment, paid time off or time to spend volunteering, and approval to change work hours or reduce work activities (Sinha, 2015). Volunteer Canada, the national association for volunteering across Canada, has been instrumental in working with industry to advance employer-supported volunteering programs, including skills-based volunteering, workplace-located volunteering such as online volunteering and micro-volunteering, and team or group volunteering (Speevak Sladowski & Kaleniecka, 2014; Volunteer Canada, 2016).

Cooperatives also operate with volunteer labor. This is sometimes called *social labor* as in some cases those contributing unpaid labor receive benefits such as reduced rent or child care costs. Industry Canada estimates that about 36,000 individuals volunteer in the operation of cooperatives and another 19,000 serve as directors. Most of these volunteers and directors are found in housing cooperatives (Industry Canada, 2018).

Almost 90% of social enterprises in a national study indicated that they had volunteers, and a third had more than thirty volunteers. In total, 1,350 reporting social enterprises indicated they involved at least 116,000 volunteers (Elson, Hall, & Wamucii, 2016).

3.3   *Participation and Informal Volunteering*
The 2013 General Social Survey also provides data on participation.[5] Two-thirds of Canadians aged fifteen and over participate in groups, organizations,

---

5   The question asked in the survey was "whether, in the past 12 months, they had been a member or participant in any of the following types of groups: 1) a union or professional

and associations (Turcotte, 2015c). The most popular of these are sports or recreational organizations (31%), followed by union or professional associations (28%), cultural, educational, or hobby organizations (20%), school, group, or neighborhood, civic or community associations (17%), and religious-affiliated groups (14%). Over half of this participation (57%) took the form of volunteering for these groups.

Across Canada, participation rates have a degree of association with volunteering rates. Provinces with higher volunteer rates are also more likely have high participation rates. The province with the highest rate of participation based on 2013 data is British Columbia at 73%, while Quebeckers participate at a rate of 58% (Turcotte, 2015c). Participation rates overall are consistent by gender overall; however, do vary type of group, organization or association (Table 3).

TABLE 3   Percentage participation in civic engagement of Canadians aged fifteen or older, gender and overall by top five groups, 2013

	Overall	Sports or recreational organizations	Union or professional associations	Cultural, educational, or hobby organizations	School group or neighborhood, civic or community associations	Religious-affiliated groups
All	65	31	28	20	17	14
Gender						
Men (ref)	66	34	28	18	15	12
Women	65	28	27	23	20	16

SOURCE: TURCOTTE (2015C), P. 23.

association; 2) a political party or group; 3) a sports or recreational organization (such as a hockey league, health club or golf club); 4) a cultural, educational or hobby organization (such as a theatre group, book club or bridge club); 5) a religious-affiliated group (such as a church youth group or choir); 6) a school group or neighborhood, civic or community association (such as PTA, alumni, block parents or neighborhood watch); 7) a service club (such as Kiwanis, Knights of Columbus or the Legion); 8) a seniors' group (such as a seniors' club, recreational association or resource center); 9) a youth organization (such as Scouts, Guides, Big Brothers, Big Sisters or the YWCA/YMCA); 10) an ethnic or immigrant association or club; 11) another type of organization" (Turcotte, 2015c, p. 21).

Participation rates vary according to stage of life, region, level of education, personal income, and immigration status (Table 4). Young people tend to participate at higher rates in general, and particularly in sports and recreational groups, and social and community groups. Seniors aged sixty-five and over tend to be involved mostly heavily with religious groups and seniors' groups. Those with higher levels of education and higher personal income participate at higher rates overall. Immigrants tend to participate at lower rates than non-immigrants.

TABLE 4   Percentage participation in civic engagement of Canadians aged fifteen or older overall, by age group, level of education, personal income, and immigrant status

	Overall
Age Group	
15 to 24	69
25 to 34	65
35 to 44 (ref)	69
45 to 54	65
55 to 64	64
65 to 74	62
75 and over	59
Level of Education	
Less than high school diploma (ref)	41
High school diploma	56
Postsecondary diploma or certificate	67
University degree	78
Personal income	
Less than $40,000 (ref)	56
$40,000 to $79,999	73
$80,000 or more	81
Immigrant status	
Non-immigrant (ref)	67
Established immigrant (before 2000)	63
Recent immigrant (between 2000 and 2013)	59

COMPILED FROM TURCOTTE (2015C), PP. 23, 24.

With the advent of the Internet, it is not surprising that Internet-related engagement as it relates to participating in groups has increased (44%) compared to ten years earlier (23%). Use of the Internet in 2013 in this regard was primarily through email, blogs, forums, or social networks (59%), sharing knowledge and information (58%), and organizing and scheduling activities (53%).

While the social economy framework takes an organization or enterprise approach, social support also happens outside of the direction of organizations. This is known as informal volunteering and can happen individually or through social groups (Einolf et al., 2016).

A particular form of civic engagement is helping others by providing care or physical labor for house or yardwork (Reed & Selbee, 2001). This includes "shoveling a senior neighbour's driveway or preparing meals for a sick colleague" (Sinha, 2015, p. 17). Often this type of direct helping activity is not seen as volunteer work because it is not done through an organization, but rather as just being neighborly (Cnaan, Handy, & Wadsworth, 1996).

Although informal volunteering is more prevalent than formal volunteering, few surveys ask about it (Einolf et al., 2016). The 2013 General Social Survey is an exception and reports that 82% of Canadians aged fifteen and older helped people directly, in other words without going through an organization or group (Sinha, 2015). This is almost double the rate of formal volunteering (44%). The most common form of helping was housework and home maintenance (59%), followed by health-related or personal care (49%), and shopping, driving to the store or to an appointment (45%).

Overall men and women helped others at similar rates; however, women were more likely to help with health-related or personal care (58% vs 40%), while men were more likely to report helping in the category of housework, outdoor work, and home maintenance (65% vs 53%). While immigrants are less likely to do formal volunteering, they are just as likely as non-immigrants to provide informal care (Wang, Mook, & Handy, 2017).

4   **Educational and Research Infrastructure Supporting the Social Economy in Canada**

In the next part of this review, we look at the supporting educational and research infrastructure for the social economy in Canada.

4.1   *Educational Infrastructure*
There is a strong set of support organizations for research and knowledge dissemination on the social economy. Some of it is specific to universities,

colleges, and the like; other parts are integrated into umbrella organizations serving a particular organization type within the social economy (e.g., foundations, charities, cooperatives, community development). Some are labeled as research centers; others as academic programs or certificates. In addition, there are courses that are not part of a specialized program, both specific to one organizational form and more general. All have the purpose of disseminating knowledge about organizations in the social economy. In this section, we provide an overview of such organizations—arguably, an educational infrastructure for Canada's social economy.

Some such organizations have a lengthy history; for example, the Co-operative College of Canada (no longer operating) was established in Saskatoon in the middle of the 20th century to promote cooperative values. It was modeled after the Co-operative College in Manchester, England, set up at the end of the First World War (MacPherson, 1979). Some of the Canadian college's functions were overtaken by the Centre for the Study of Cooperatives (CSC) at the University of Saskatchewan, established in 1984 (CSC, 2018). CSC was one of the earlier academic units in universities across Canada supporting organizations in the social economy.

Interestingly, with the odd exception, most of the education programs focus on a particular organization form (nonprofit or cooperative) or types of activity that bridge various organization forms (community economic development, community development, social entrepreneurship). We subdivide the overview into organizations operating in institutions of higher education and community-based organizations, some in partnership with universities and colleges. We focus on programs related to cooperatives, community development, and nonprofit organizations, though others such as social entrepreneurship and leadership could be included too. The examples that follow are primarily from anglophone Canada.

4.1.1 University and College Programs

There are many programs in universities and colleges related to the social economy. Some programs and centers in universities and colleges are sponsored by large corporations in the social economy plus the university itself. The Centre for the Study of Cooperatives at the University of Saskatchewan (referred to above) is sponsored by a group of large cooperatives: Federated Cooperatives Limited, The Co-operators, Concentra, and CHS Inc. It is a multidisciplinary center that draws faculty from different departments across the University of Saskatchewan engaged in research and teaching about cooperatives. CSC is also associated with an interdisciplinary graduate concentration in cooperative studies and a graduate certificate in the social economy and cooperatives (Hancock & Brault, 2016).

CSC is one of a group of higher education initiatives across Canada devoted to co-ops. Among the better known are:

- the St. Mary's University (Halifax), Master of Management and Cooperatives and Credit Unions and their Graduate Diploma in Cooperative Management, which touts itself as a "different type of targeted and advanced business education that recognizes the unique social value cooperative models bring to business" (http://www.smu.ca/academics/sobey/sobey -cooperative-management-education.html);
- the Master's in Management and Governance of Cooperatives and Mutuals at l'Institut de recherche et d'éducation pour les coopératives et les mutuelles de l'Université de Sherbrooke (IRECUS)—"The program aims to challenge traditional enterprise models and presents alternatives that put people and the community at the center of the enterprise" (http://www .smu.ca/webfiles/IRECUSprofile.pdf).

There are also higher education programs devoted to the field of community development (CD). The Coady International Institute in St. Francis Xavier University was an offshoot of the Antigonish Movement (named after the local community in Nova Scotia) focusing on community development in response to the Great Depression and the poverty that preceded it (https:// www.stfx.ca/coady-institute). The movement was led by Fathers Moses Coady and Jimmy Tompkins and utilized adult education principles as a form of local mobilization. In 1928, the university asked Dr. Coady to establish an extension department that would focus on community outreach. The Antigonish Movement led to the development of credit unions and fishery co-ops in the Atlantic and also to the Coady International Institute, started in 1959. The Institute trains people from the Global South to take on leadership roles in their home country. Coady uses an asset-based approach to community development that builds on the strengths of local communities and helps animators within those communities to strengthen their community. The participants in its program are from all over the Global South—for example, Vietnam, South Africa, Ethiopia, Zambia, and Ghana.

The Coady International Institute is engaged in participatory research and development within a local–global framework. Another similar arrangement in Canada is the Knowledge for Change (K4C) Global Consortium, which is a partnership between the University of Victoria and the Society for Participatory Research in Asia (PRIA) (http://www.pria.org). The K4C Global Consortium offers an online Mentor Training Programme for both Canadian and international participatory researchers interested in learning how to teach participatory research.

There are other CED and CD programs in universities across Canada. Some offer Master's degrees or a graduate diploma—for example:

- Cape Breton University has a Master's in Business Administration in Community Economic Development, operating not only in Sydney but also across Canada;
- the University of Victoria School of Public Administration houses a Master of Arts in Community Development (MACD) and a Diploma in Indigenous Community Development and Governance;
- Concordia University has a graduate diploma in community economic development;
- the University of Toronto has a Collaborative Master's Specialization in Community Development bringing together faculty and students from five graduate programs (the Program in Planning in Geography, Public Health Science, Social Work, Adult Education and Community Development, and Counselling Psychology).

Others offer a certificate: Simon Fraser University in Vancouver has a certificate program in Community Economic Development (CED) and Dalhousie does as well.

The Directory of Post-Secondary Programs Related to CED lists about forty such initiatives (https://www.ccednet-rcdec.ca/en/page/directory-post-secondary-programs-related-ced). Some are referred to as community economic development; others are variations of that theme. We organize them by undergrad, Master's, and certificate. Interestingly, there is very little at the doctoral level—only Indigenous Studies, Trent University, and Adult Education and Community Development, University of Toronto, suggesting that these are primarily non-research degrees. Some select examples follow:

- **Undergrad (BA):** Community Economic and Social Development, Algoma University; Rural and Community Studies, Brandon University; International Development Studies, Menno Simons College; Social Development Studies, Renison University College; Urban and Inner-City Studies, University of Winnipeg;
- **College Diploma:** Community Economic and Social Development, Algoma University; Community Worker, George Brown College; Business Admin & Community Economic Development Stream, Aurora College; International Development Studies; Community Studies, College of the North Atlantic; Aboriginal Community Advocacy, Confederation College; Menno Simmons College; Community Worker—Outreach & Development, Sheridan College; Recreation and Community Development, Saskatchewan Polytechnic;

- **Master's:** City Planning, University of Manitoba; Social Enterprise & Entrepreneurship, Memorial University; Social Enterprise Leadership MBA, University of Fredericton;
- **Certificate:** Local Government and Community Economic Development, Dalhousie University; Aboriginal Community Economic Development, Nicola Valley Institute of Technology; Responsible Leadership, Queen's University; First Nations Governance, University of Lethbridge; Local Economic Development, University of Waterloo.

The largest group of higher education programs related to the social economy is devoted to nonprofit organizations. In a recent study, Sulek and Mirabella (forthcoming) state that there are seventy-four programs in sixty-eight post-secondary education institutions that include nonprofit and/or philanthropic studies in their curriculum. The Schulich School of Business at York University was one of the early ones, started in 1983, and has a Nonprofit Management and Leadership Program within its MBA as well as a Post Graduate Diploma. Now titled the Social Sector Management Program, it has expanded to include Social Entrepreneurship, Social Finance, and Social Impact Investing. There are similar opportunities in the undergraduate program. Schulich also offers professional management certificates from time to time (for example, in partnership with the Ontario Cooperative Association, the United Way, and various foundations) as well as custom-designed leadership programs (public housing, the child welfare sector, health systems).

As with cooperatives, many of the nonprofit higher education programs were started with the support of foundations and other organizations in the social economy. However, some of these programs proved to be vulnerable, and in many cases did not endure once the funding period was ended (Sulek & Mirabella, forthcoming). It is unclear why some programs collapsed, but one might surmise that unless the university has a core faculty committed to such a program, it would be at risk. Other reasons may be that enrolments were insufficient for the program to be self-supporting and that external nonprofit organizations lacked the resources to support them (Personal Communication, Vic Murray, June 18, 2018).

Imagine Canada (formerly the Canadian Centre for Philanthropy) organized a series of programs in the 1980s in conjunction with colleges across Canada in Fundraising Management, Non-Profit Management, and Volunteer Management. The colleges involved were Humber and George Brown in Toronto; Mount Royal College in Calgary, Grant MacEwan College in Edmonton, Vancouver Community College and the British Columbia Institute for Technology (BCIT) in Vancouver. Not all have endured, but it was a major step forward in creating an educational infrastructure.

The McConnell Foundation helped to sponsor the McGill-McConnell Program for National Voluntary Sector Leaders in the 1990s, but it did not continue beyond the initial funding period. The Kahanoff Foundation funded a 'Third Sector and Public Policy' program at Queen's University School of Policy from 2000 to 2005, but it too did not survive. The Institute for Nonprofit Studies, supported by private philanthropy, started an undergrad program in Nonprofit Management, and this has been taken over the Bissett School of Business at Mount Royal and morphed into a Bachelor of Business Administration with a nonprofit stream.

Two important initiatives in the past decade in the creation of higher education programs regarding nonprofits were the Master of Philanthropy and Nonprofit Leadership degree and graduate diploma programs at Carleton University's School of Public Policy and Administration in 2012 and the Bachelor of Nonprofit Management and Leadership Studies at Western University's Brescia University College, in London, Ontario. A key difference between these programs and some earlier initiatives is that they were driven by key faculty within the university rather than external forces. The Carleton program is housed within School of Public Policy and Administration (SPPA); Western's, very recent, is housed within the School of Leadership and Social Change.

In addition to degree programs, there are many certificate programs concerning nonprofits and related topics, as outlined on the Charity Village website (https://charityvillage.com/cms/active-learning/related-links/post -secondary-nonprofit-programs). These include:

- Ryerson University: Certificate in Nonprofit and Voluntary Sector Management;
- Simon Fraser University: Nonprofit Management Certificate (online);
- British Columbia Institute of Technology (BCIT): Nonprofit Management Associate Certificate Program;
- Kwantlen Polytechnic University: NGO and Nonprofit Studies;
- Mount Royal University Faculty of Continuing Education: Nonprofit Management Certificate;
- University of Ontario, Institute of Technology: Not-for-Profit Management Certificate Program;
- Western University Continuing Studies: Not-for-Profit Management Certificate Program.

In addition, a recent initiative is the Certificate in Nonprofit Sector Leadership and Innovation at Luther College, University of Regina.

There are other certificate programs related to nonprofits focused on a specific activity, for example:

– **Fundraising** (e.g.: Algonquin College: Certificate in Fundraising Management; British Columbia Institute of Technology (BCIT): Fundraising Management Certificate Program; Fanshawe College: Fundraising Certificate; George Brown College: Fundraising Certificate; Ryerson University: Certificate in Fundraising Management);

– **Leadership** (e.g.: Conestoga College: Senior Leadership and Management in the Not-For-Profit Sector; Dalhousie University: Non-Profit Sector Leadership Program; Mohawk College: Not-for-Profit Leadership Development Certificate Program; Nova Scotia Community College: Nonprofit Leadership Program; Seneca College: Nonprofit Leadership & Management Graduate Certificate; Summit Pacific College: Not For Profit Organizational Leadership Program);

– **International Development** (e.g.: Tyndale University College: Bachelor of Arts in Business Administration/International Development).

4.1.2   Dissertations and Theses

A study of master and doctoral theses completed from 1970 to 2012 at Canadian universities found that an average of ten per year were published related to cooperatives (Thériault, 2014). In more recent years (2005 to 2012), these numbered eleven to fifteen. Almost 60% of these were published in universities located in Quebec, and more than a third had an international focus. The average age of those completing master's theses was thirty-three at the time of publication, while the average age for those completing doctoral theses was thirty-nine. In general, the theses are not pursuing theoretical issues and many take a case study approach.

A similar study of dissertations and theses on other social economy topics is yet to be done. However, in reviewing dissertations and theses written on topics related to formal nonprofit organizations included in the database *Proquest Dissertation and Theses* in 2011/12, including ones published at Canadian universities, Shier and Handy (2014) identified five analytic categories or themes: (1) human/financial resources, for example philanthropy and volunteerism; (2) effectiveness/performance, including accountability, organizational effectiveness, and efficiency; (3) organization development including organization behavior and the legal and policy context; (4) intra-organization context, including governance, leadership, and management; and (5) inter-organization context including collaboration and government relationships. According to Shier and Handy (2014), analysis of the five-year period of 2006 to 2010 shows that the most prevalent topic is organization development, followed by intra-organizational context, inter-organization context, resources, and effectiveness/performance.

4.1.3 Non-formal Education in Social Economy Organizations

The social economy is clustered around organizations with similar services and within each cluster there is usually an umbrella organization that creates educational services for members. This is non-formal education because it is external to the formal education system, though often it involves accreditation of some sort (Livingstone, 1999; Schugurensky, 2000). Many of these programs operate below the radar and are known to participants in the organizational cluster, but not broadly. For example, cooperatives have an umbrella organization based on the type of service that they offer, and these organizations operate non-formal educational services. Here are some select examples:

- Cooperative Housing Federation of Toronto offers a series of workshops for co-op staff—Preparing for your board meeting; Preventative maintenance; Living through capital projects (CHFT, 2018).
- The Credit Union Institute of Canada, owned by the Canadian Credit Union Association, offers a twelve-part course for credit union employees who are preparing for management positions. Graduates are awarded the designation "Associate of the Credit Union Institute of Canada" (Credit Union Institute, 2018).
- The Canadian Credit Union Association also offers the Credit Union Director Achievement (CUDA) Program with three levels of programs: Foundations of Governance, Governance in Action, and Governance Application. The graduates of these programs become Accredited Canadian Credit Union Director (CCUA, 2018a).
- Co-op Zone, a network of co-op developers offers a series of courses to facilitate the development of cooperatives (http://www.coopzone.coop/Courses/).
- Imagine Canada offers accreditation through its Standards program, designed to help charities and other nonprofits to strengthen their practices. In total there are seventy-three standards organized into five groups: board of governance; financial accountability and transparency; fundraising; staff management; and volunteer involvement. The Standards program, which was started in 2012, was set up in consultation with Volunteer Canada and the HR (human resource) Council, as well as after meetings with leaders of Canadian charities and other nonprofits (Imagine Canada, 2018).
- Community Foundations of Canada offers its member organizations (community foundations in 191 communities across Canada) leadership training planned with the Carold Institute. The program is "designed to offer full-time community foundation staff new skills and knowledge to enhance their leadership, strengthen their organization, and contribute to the movement and their communities in new ways" (Community Foundations of Canada, 2018a).

There are also community economic development programs offered by community organizations. For example:

- the Economic Developers Association of Alberta offers a series of CED-related programs (http://www.edaalberta.ca/page-68187);
- Cando (Council for the Advancement of Native Development Officers) is a federally registered, nonprofit society that is Aboriginal controlled, community based, and membership driven. Cando focuses on the education, professional development and certification of economic development officers in Aboriginal communities (http://www.edo.ca/certification).

These comprise but a select list of non-formal education programs offered. They are widespread and very much a norm among apex organizations in the social economy who try to serve a membership.

4.2 Associations Supporting Research on the Social Economy Sector in Canada

As with education programs, professional associations are tied primarily to organizational forms, though the Association for Nonprofit and Social Economy Research (ANSER) does attempt to bridge the entire social economy. In addition, Canadian researchers are engaged in international organizations—for example, ARNOVA in the US; CIRIEC in Western Europe and more broadly; and ISTR (International Society for Third-Sector Research). In this section, we focus on the Canadian associations, but mention the others because Canadian researchers participate in them.[6]

Research related to the social economy is organized both by associations that are primarily academic and by associations that are community based. In the latter case, the research is likely to be tied to policy. This section, therefore, is subdivided accordingly.

4.2.1 Academic Associations

Academic associations in Canada generally meet as part of the Congress for the Humanities and Social Sciences, a federation, started in 1938. The Congress is a federation of 80 academic associations (in 2018) plus universities from across Canada that meets annually at one of the member universities, typically the last week of May and the beginning of June (https://www.ideas-idees.ca/events/congress). Not all associations meet as part of every Congress, usually there are sixty-five to seventy-five (Personal Communication, Donna Lelievre, June 15, 2018). The associations range from those that are large and general such as the Canadian Sociological Association and the Canadian Political

---

6   For an overview of the growth of academic associations worldwide, see Smith (2013, 2016).

Science Association (CPSA) to those that are very small and specialized such as the Finno-Ugric Studies Association of Canada (FUSAC) and the Folklore Studies Association of Canada (FSAC). Academics, graduate students, and community researchers engaged in social economy research can present at any association that accepts their proposal. There are two associations focus on research related to the social economy: the Association for Nonprofit and Social Economy Research (ANSER) and the Canadian Association for the Study of Co-operation (CASC).

4.2.1.1   *Canadian Association for Studies in Co-operation*
CASC was started in 1982 by professors Ian MacPherson (University of Victoria) and Jack Craig (York University) and focuses on cooperatives (including credit unions and other associations with similar structures) and more broadly on economic and social cooperation. It is a specialized, relatively small association sustained through support from the Centre for the Study of Cooperatives, Universities of Saskatchewan; Cooperatives and Mutuals Canada (formerly, the Canadian Cooperative Association); and the BC Institute for Cooperative Studies at the University of Victoria (no longer operating). One of CASC's fundamental purposes has been to promote research and education on cooperatives and engage officials in the cooperative sector and in government agencies that deal with cooperatives, alongside interested academics and students. Collaboration with federal agencies—for example, the Cooperatives Secretariat and the Rural Secretariat (both no longer operating) have been important to CASC.

CASC is primarily an anglophone association though on occasion it has reached out to francophone colleagues in Quebec, for example, through organizing joint conferences with CIRIEC-Canada and IRECUS-Université de Sherbrooke. CASC organizes joint events with other associations both within the Congress and externally—for example, the Association of Cooperative Educators (ACE), a predominantly US association, and the International Cooperative Alliance's Committee on Cooperative Research, an international network of researchers of cooperatives. CASC serves as the Canadian distributor of the British publication, *Journal of Co-operative Studies*.

In 2006 and 2007, there was an effort by some members to broaden CASC to include researchers of nonprofits and the social economy. There was resistance within CASC, largely concerns about being swamped by a larger group and weakening the association's connection to cooperative research and education as well as agencies and government officials. This led to the creation of the Association for Nonprofit and Social Economy Research (ANSER) in 2008 (see the next section). CASC normally meets about the same time as ANSER at the Congress, there are some joint sessions, and a shared banquet. Otherwise, the associations—substantially overlapping as ANSER too includes researchers of cooperatives and CASC includes more broadly than cooperatives—operate independently of each other, each having its own executive committee and members, though some people belong to both associations.

4.2.1.2   Association for Nonprofit and Social Economy Research

As explained above, ANSER was organized after CASC declined to restructure itself. The organizing for ANSER began in the fall of 2007, initially by a group of six who were either part of CASC or who were engaged in the research networks that had been spawned across Canada with funding for social economy research by the Social Sciences and Humanities Research Council of Canada (SSHRC). The founding group (Peter Elson, Michael Hall, Laurie Mook, Vic Murray, Jack Quarter, and Keith Seel) arranged for status as a member association within the Federation of the Congress for Humanities and Social Sciences and used their available research networks to promote the new association. The decision to operate within the Congress system was in part because an earlier effort to organize an association for nonprofit researchers was unsuccessful, and it was decided that it was too challenging for a volunteer association to organize an annual conference on its own.

The first ANSER conference at the Congress at the University of British Columbia, June 4–6, 2008, had over a hundred registrants. At that first conference, ANSER was organized more officially, and a steering committee was set up; the first board became official once incorporation was achieved on March 9, 2010. A charitable registration was attained four years later, on January 30, 2014. ANSER established the *Canadian Journal of Nonprofit and Social Economy Research* (ANSERJ) in 2010, an online open-source publication, which publishes two volumes each year.

ANSER refers to itself as a "Canadian association for those who have an interest in research that pertains broadly to nonprofit organizations and the social economy" (http://www.anser-ares.ca/about-us/). The intent of the founders was to have a bilingual association and the French-language name (Association de recherche sur les organismes sans but lucratif et de l'économie sociale, and acronym, ARES) was displayed prominently on the association's website, correspondence, and journal. However, bilingualism has proven challenging, not just for ANSER but also for Canadian associations in general. The ANSER journal publishes its abstracts in both languages, and occasionally there are French-language submissions; however, the ANSER board has had difficulty recruiting members from Quebec and participants from Quebec are under-represented in the board and membership.

An analysis of ANSER's conference presentations during the first ten years indicates that just over a third were on nonprofit organizations and topics; about one-sixth were on the social economy; about one-eighth on social enterprises and a similar portion on cooperatives. There were also presentations on civil society and inter-sectoral issues (Mook & Theriault, 2018).

ANSER's registrations were higher during its first four years because of large research funding for the social economy from SSHRC. Once this funding ended, the registrations have settled in about 100, higher when the Congress is in Central Canada and lower when it is elsewhere (Mook & Theriault, 2018).

Conference registrants are mainly from universities and also include many graduate students. ANSER gives awards to students for the best master's and doctoral theses and grants some travel subsidies. About one-quarter of the participants at annual conferences are community researchers—some from agencies, others independent.

ANSER is financially independent, earning most of its revenues from registrations at its annual conferences. It also receives sponsorships from external organizations such as Alterna Credit Union and related university centers. In its formative period, ANSER was assisted by funding and staff support from the Institute for Nonprofit Studies at Mount Royal University in Calgary and by the Social Economy Centre at the University of Toronto.

4.2.2   Non-Academic, Community-Based Associations

There are many examples of associations related to the social economy's functioning across Canada. If the screen we applied were nonprofit associations, there would be thousands. Instead we use as a screen nonprofit and cooperative umbrella associations whose primary activities are engaged in developing the social economy, including a research component, often policy research.

4.2.2.1   *CCEDNet: Canadian CED Network*

In Canada, there is an active network of practitioners engaged in community economic development (CED) that coalesces around the umbrella organization CCEDNet (https://www.ccednet-rcdec.ca/en). There are also some regional CCEDNet affiliates such as the Manitoba CED Network. The CED network has a lengthy history in Canada, going back at least to the formation of the first community development corporation: New Dawn in Sydney in 1976. From that point forward, many other community development corporations were developed—for example, Community Ownership Solutions and Build in Winnipeg; Station 20 West, Saskatoon; Street Youth Job Action, Vancouver; and the Learning Enrichment Foundation in Toronto. Much of the CED in Canada is tied to government regional development programs and funding for workplace integration of members of marginalized social groups (e.g., youth, homeless) (Quarter, Mook, & Armstrong, 2018). Recently, activities of CCEDNet members have focused on work integration social enterprises for marginalized social groups.

CCEDNet was incorporated in 1999, but there was a history of association among the members preceding that. Although the members interact in various ways during the year, it has held an annual conference each spring for most of the period from 2001 to the present. The organization has just over 200 members, including large organizations such as Cooperatives and Mutuals Canada. The primary activity of CCEDNet and affiliates is the development of local communities, often in lower-income areas, but the network also engages in research primarily contracted with government agencies and often with a policy orientation.

4.2.2.2   *Cooperatives and Mutuals Canada (CMC)*

There are many associations in Canada for cooperatives. The primary umbrella organization is Cooperatives and Mutuals Canada (CMC), formerly the Canadian Cooperative Association.

CMC defines its mission as: "Cooperatives and Mutuals Canada (CMC) is a member-driven association that supports, promotes and unites cooperative and mutual organisations. CMC strives to advance the cooperative economy by organizing co-op development, advocating with government and conducting research to improve public policy (http://canada.coop/en/about-cmc)."

CMC has about fifty members including affiliates in provinces across Canada (e.g., Newfoundland—Labrador Federation of Cooperatives; Conseil québécois de la coopération et la mutualité), affiliates by co-op sectors (Canadian Credit Union Association, Canadian Worker Cooperative Federation); and large cooperatives from across Canada (Federated Cooperatives Ltd., The Co-operators Group). Together with its affiliates, CMC strives to represent the interests of cooperatives to government, the public, and other interested parties. CMC is an affiliate of the International Cooperative Alliance, the umbrella organization for cooperatives internationally. Among its primary activities are assisting the development of cooperatives and researching policy issues in a manner that meets the interests of its members.

4.2.2.3   *Canadian Credit Union Association (CCUA) and the Desjardins Group*

Credit unions in Canada are a form of cooperative association, but they also operate within separate federations. The Canadian Credit Union Association (CCUA) refers to itself as "the national credit union trade association, representing credit unions, caisses populaires (outside of Quebec) and regional credit union Central organizations" (https://www.ccua.com/about). The regional centrals (e.g., Atlantic Central, SaskCentral) also operate as trade associations for their locales and manage liquidity reserves and provide other banking and related services to credit unions in their respective regions. In addition to the CCUA representing credit unions outside of Quebec, le Mouvement Desjardins (the Desjardins Group) serves a similar function for caisses populaires in Quebec and also in other parts of francophone Canada. Taken as a total system, there are 567 credit unions/caisses populaires in Canada with 2,787 branches, more than 10.3 million members, and more than $391 billion of assets (Personal Communication, Kevin Morris, June 19, 2018; CCUA, 2018c). The CCUA and Desjardins are the political voices for these associations; they engage in policy research and financial support for the locals.

4.2.3   Nonprofit Associations

Unlike cooperatives that generally have a strong identity related to their form of incorporation, nonprofits tend to identify more with form of service—for example, BC Non-profit Housing Association, Ontario Coalition for Better Childcare, Canadian Labour Congress, etc. Nevertheless, there are important umbrella associations related to the sector that we briefly discuss.

4.2.3.1   *Ontario Nonprofit Network (ONN)*

Most nonprofit umbrella organizations are related to a particular organizational form (e.g., charities, foundations), but ONN differs in that it relates to the entirety of nonprofits in Ontario. Its website proclaims that ONN is an "independent network for the 58,000 nonprofits in Ontario, focused on policy, advocacy, and services to strengthen Ontario's nonprofit sector as a key pillar of our society and economy" (http://theonn.ca/our-network/).

ONN began in 2007 in response to changes in the province's "not-for-profit" legislation (Bill 65) and officially incorporated in 2014. The association engages actively in policy research and is a strong advocate for the interests of nonprofits in general and for specific forms of nonprofits through its working groups. For example, ONN has lobbied for Ontario to implement a strong social procurement strategy that would be of benefit to nonprofit organizations and emphasize "community benefits" in its Infrastructure for Jobs and Prosperity Act, 2015, and the 2017 Long-Term Infrastructure Plan.

4.2.3.2   *Imagine Canada*

Imagine Canada began in 2005 as a result of a merger of the Canadian Centre for Philanthropy and the Coalition of National Voluntary Organizations (NVO).

The latter was a public-sector nonprofit, funded by various government departments, that was registered in 1998, and lobbied government on behalf of the charities until 2005 (Government of Canada, 2018). The Canadian Centre for Philanthropy started in 1981, and although much of its research was funded by government, it operated more independently from government than the NVO. Its goals were: "to collect and disseminate information; to generate research and publications; to train and develop skills within the sector; and to inform the public and the government about the role and importance of philanthropy" (Philanthropist Editors, 2000, p. 1). One undertaking of the Canadian Centre for Philanthropy, until 1986, was to be the publisher of Philanthropist, a journal serving charitable organizations. Imagine Canada lobbies Canadian governments on behalf of charities in Canada, engages in research both on its own and in conjunction with Statistics Canada and other government agencies (e.g., the National Survey of Giving, Volunteering and Participating). It has an innovative Standards program that certifies charities and other nonprofits who are able to meet acceptable standards in their board governance, financial accountability and transparency, fundraising, staff management, and volunteer involvement (http://www.imaginecanada.ca/our-programs/standards-program/standards).

4.2.3.3   *Volunteer Canada*

Volunteer Canada refers to itself as the "national voice for volunteerism in Canada" (https://volunteer.ca/index.php?MenuItemID=317). Since 1977, it has served as the umbrella organization for volunteer centers across Canada that act as an intermediary by matching members of the public with suitable volunteer placements in nonprofit organizations. Some of Volunteer Canada's members are provincial (Volunteer Manitoba, Volunteer BC), some are big-city (Volunteer Ottawa, Volunteer Halifax), and some are small communities (Volunteer Cowichan, Volunteer Campbell River). Some United Ways are members and some members use variations of the name (Sarnia Gives, Pillar Nonprofit Network).

Volunteer Canada endeavors to increase volunteering and civic participation through organizing events for corporations and the public and creates resources that its members can use: for example, a volunteer management handbook, a resource guide for working volunteers with disabilities, and a handbook for employer-sponsored volunteering. It takes a leading role in National Volunteer Week and various other activities that promote volunteering in Canada.

4.2.3.4   *Philanthropic Foundations Canada (PFC)*

PFC is a primary voice for private and public foundations and other forms of grant-makers in Canada. Its members are among the largest foundations in Canada and represent a strong voice "by encouraging public policies that sustain the sector, by increasing awareness of philanthropy's contribution to the well-being of Canadians, and by providing opportunities for funders to learn from each other" (https://pfc.ca/about/). PFC was founded in 1999 and became a registered charity in 2002. The head office in Montreal generates policy documents that increase public awareness of foundations and those that serve as helpful information to researchers and government policy developers. These include: Snapshot of Foundation Giving in 2015, November 2017; Assets and Giving of Canada's Top Grantmaking Foundations; and Assets & Giving Trends of Canada's Grantmaking Foundations, September 2014. PFC's values statement emphasizes that its member foundations are "individually and collectively committed to the public good" (https://pfc.ca/wp-content/uploads/2018/02/statement-of-values-2018-en.pdf).

4.2.3.5   *Community Foundations of Canada (CFC)*

A prominent subset of public foundations in Canada is the community foundation, endowed grant-making organizations that are designed to serve the needs of a geographic community. The umbrella organization for Canada's 191 community foundations is Community Foundations of Canada (CFC). The largest community foundations are in our large urban centers: Vancouver, Winnipeg, Calgary, Edmonton, Victoria, Toronto, Hamilton, Ottawa, and Montreal. However, community foundations also blanket small communities across Canada—for example, Battlefords and District Community Foundation; Thompson Community Foundation; Fundy Community Foundation. One of CFC's most important initiatives is its Vital Signs program, used by foundations across Canada and internationally. These annual reports prepared by community foundations involve the analysis of data to assess the quality of life in specific communities on such indicators as poverty, food security, and youth unemployment (http://communityfoundations.ca/our-work/vital-signs/). The intent is to inform policy and priorities that can be utilized to address these problems.

4.2.4   Social Enterprises

Social enterprises operate in many forms. Some are profit-oriented businesses that are focused on creating a form of social good, while others are nonprofit associations. Of the nonprofit associations, some are associated with the CCEDNet network and others are incorporated as cooperatives and participate in related associations. Nevertheless, there are associations that are specific to social enterprises and we briefly present those here.

4.2.4.1   MaRS

The MaRS Discovery District in Toronto's mission is to "work with entrepreneurs and investors to launch and grow companies that have broad economic and societal impact" (https://www.marsdd.com/about/story/). One part of MaRS is its national initiative Social Innovation Generation (SiG), which assists the development of social enterprises, including nonprofits. MaRS not only operates as a hub for their development but also as a network for their ongoing association with each other. SiG is supported by J. W. McConnell Family Foundation and the Province of Ontario.

4.2.4.2   Social Enterprise Council of Canada (SECC)

Like MaRS, SECC is both a development hub and a network association. It defines itself as "an alliance of social enterprise leaders who leverage their networks, knowledge and experience in order to build a strong and enabling environment for social enterprise" (http://secouncil.ca/index.php/about/). It organizes conferences of social enterprises in Canada and develops policy documents that are designed to improve government programs.

4.2.4.3   Chantier de l'économie sociale

Within Quebec, le Chantier de l'économie sociale serves a similar function to both SiG at MaRS and SECC, in so far as it is both a development entity and an association. The key feature to le Chantier's program is its trust fund (Fiducie du Chantier de l'économie sociale, or the Chantier Trust), endowed initially by a grant from the Federal Government in 2005 under its social economy program (Mendell & Rouzier, 2006). Through the trust, le Chantier provides "patient capital" to small social enterprises that remain part of its network.

4.2.4.4   Centre for Social Innovation

CSI, with three locations in Toronto and one in New York, defines itself as a space where social entrepreneurs and innovators can locate and generate synergies through interacting with each other. CSI bridges nonprofits and profit-oriented enterprises.

4.2.4.5   Other Social Enterprise Associations

In addition to these development groups/associations, the social enterprise field is populated by many networks, often regionally based. These include: the BC Centre for Social Enterprise; Social Enterprise Network of Nova Scotia; Social Enterprise Ontario; Ontario Social Economy Roundtable; Social Enterprise Toronto, and so on. Many of these associations (e.g., Social Enterprise Canada) are embedded within other larger organizations such as CCEDNet.

In addition, there are also support organizations specific to social enterprises that also serve as associations. These include: the Toronto Enterprise Fund; School for Social Entrepreneurs; and the Canadian Social Entrepreneurship Foundation.

4.3   *Research Funding Bodies*

In Canada, the primary funder of research in the social sciences and humanities is the Social Sciences and Humanities Research Council of Canada—SSHRC, as it is known. SSHRC is an agency within the Government of Canada that was legislated in 1977 and reports to Parliament through the Minister of Science (http://www.sshrc-crsh.gc.ca/about-au_sujet/index-eng.aspx).   Even   though SSHRC is a federal government agency, it is governed by a council consisting of members of the academic community. SSHRC's adjudication process for grants is based on peer reviews, both in English and French, through its adjudication committees and its external assessments. Put simply, the evaluation process for SSHRC grants is based on academics evaluating each other's work through a blind peer-review process. According to SSHRC's reports, for the academic year 2016–2017, 708 academics participated voluntarily in ninety-four review committees for 13,000 proposals including some oriented to student funding (SSHRC, 2018). SSHRC's adjudication process is exhaustive and is both supported and respected by members of the academic community in Canada, as is the external assessment process.

SSHRC has many different programs including some that are for student funding (doctoral fellowships, post-doctoral fellowships, master's and doctoral scholarships). However, its primary function is funding of research in the social sciences and humanities.

Of the research that is funded through the social sciences and humanities, the part that is of greatest interest to this paper is that directed toward the social economy. Over the years, this has occurred in differing ways including grants for research related to specific topics. However, from 2005 to 2010, SSHRC funded a specialized program called the Social Economy Suite that was designed to build networks of researchers in this field.

4.3.1   Social Economy Suite

In 2005, the Government of Canada announced a special allocation of funding to assist the development of the social economy. The largest part of this funding was intended for the development of community organizations to facilitate the development of the social economy, for example, the funding to le Chantier de l'économie sociale to set up a trust fund to provide patient capital for social enterprises (Quarter, Mook, & Armstrong, 2018). However, the government also allocated funds to SSHRC to assist the creation of an increased research capacity on the social economy, and this led to a network of projects across Canada referred to as the Social Economy Suite.

The projects related to the Social Economy Suite were adjudicated through SSHRC's Partnership Grants program, a research program in which academics and community partners engage in research that is of joint benefit (http://www.sshrc-crsh.gc.ca/funding-financement/programs-programmes/ partnership_grants_stage1-subventions_partenariat_etape1-eng.aspx). These grants were administered from universities across Canada—Mount St. Vincent in Halifax, l'Université du Québec à Montréal (UQAM), University of Toronto, Lakehead University, and University of Saskatchewan. An additional grant was awarded to the Canadian CED Network (CEDNet), undertaken together with universities in Western Canada. Although each of the grants was for independent research teams, an effort was made to coordinate the undertaking through the Social Economy Hub at the University of Victoria. Overall, seventy-nine universities and over 140 community organizations were involved, and the partnerships created hundreds of published journal articles, student theses, conference presentations, popular press articles, and research reports (Thompson & Emmanuel, 2012).

Some of these grants led to the creation of new research centers, for example, the Social Economy Centre at the University of Toronto; others strengthened existing centers, including the Centre for the Study of Cooperatives, University of Saskatchewan, and the BC Institute of Cooperative Studies at the University of Victoria. As noted in the section on Associations, the social economy grants led to the creation of the Association for Nonprofit and Social Economy Research (ANSER) and the strengthening of the Canadian Association for the Study of Co-operation. In brief, there was increased funding for research and for conference presentations. The funding also led to the creation of the *Canadian Journal of Nonprofit and Social Economy Research*, as part of ANSER. Some of these structural changes have endured; others have been transformed or fallen by the wayside once the funding stopped. Nevertheless, there are relatively strong networks of researchers related to the social economy across Canada, mostly in universities but also in community organizations and government. Because of the SSHRC funding, the field received credit and credibility.

4.3.2   Other Sources of Research Funding

In addition to SSHRC, which is the primary funder of social economy research in Canada, some funding comes from other levels of government and from foundations. For example, Employment and Social Development Canada, a federal agency, recently funded a series of projects evaluating the effectiveness of work integration social enterprises (WISES), both at universities and at community organizations. Similarly, the Entrepreneurship and Social Enterprise Services Unit of the Ontario Government has funded research on the measurement of social value, as it pertains to social enterprises. The J. W. McConnell Family Foundation in Montreal, one of the larger foundations in Canada, has been a key player in the funding for Social Innovation Generation (SiG), together with the Waterloo Institute for Social Innovation and Resilience, the MaRS Discover District and the PLAN Institute. SiG is primarily a development program with a research component. The Trico Charitable Foundation in Calgary specializes in funding projects related to social entrepreneurship including the funding of case studies from across Canada on innovative social enterprises. Other players in this field in Canada are the Canadian Social Entrepreneurship Foundation and the Ontario Trillium Foundation.

An important form of research that foundations are engaged in is the production of Vital Signs reports by community foundations across Canada. These documents involve analyses of communities that the foundations are embedded within. In the words of Community Foundations of Canada (2018b), "*Vital Signs* reports are used to measure community well-being, start conversations with local leaders, and identify trends to help communities act on priorities such as poverty, food insecurity, youth unemployment and more."

Most foundations and government grants are for applied work, but they can include a research component. SSHRC, however, is focused on research, and has been the primary driver of research related to the social economy.

5   Summary

This review provides a high-level overview of Canada's social economy, which includes organizations such as nonprofits, cooperatives and social enterprises: "The social economy bridges the many different types of self-governing organizations that are guided by their social objectives in the goods and services that they offer" (Quarter, Mook, & Armstrong, 2018, p. 4). Using a Venn diagram (Figure 1), we highlighted the interactions between the different sectors in society and emphasized that the social economy is an integral part of a mixed economy that serves in many ways as its social infrastructure. We find four different types of social economy organizations:

- Social Economy Businesses funded primarily by exchanging goods and services for revenues in the private sector, with limited dependence on public sector funding;
- Community Economic Development organizations typically funded by governments at early stages and by the private sector when they become economically independent;
- Public Sector Nonprofits funded primarily by governments (municipal, provincial, or federal); and
- Civil Society Organizations funded by members and donors, many of which operate with a significant volunteer labor contribution.

We looked next at the significant scope and size of the social economy in Canada, focusing on nonprofits, cooperatives, and social enterprises. This led to an overview of the scope of voluntaristic behaviors; in particular, giving, volunteering, and participating.

Following this, we described the infrastructure that supports research of the sector. This included key academic and umbrella associations, as well as formal and informal educational programs. We also highlighted key funders who provide resources to support research.

As we conclude this article, the United Nations is releasing its updated statistical guidance document. *Satellite Account on Nonprofit and Related Institutions and Volunteer Work* (United Nations, 2018). This is a major shift from the previous document issued in 2002, which focused only on nonprofits and volunteering. It now highlights collecting data on what it calls the Third or Social Economy Sector (TSE), thus facilitating more insights into the social economy as a comprehensive sector, rather than having to piece together bits and pieces about nonprofit organizations, cooperatives, and social enterprises as we have had to do in the past. We look forward to the first reporting under these guidelines, and the furthering of the social economy concept.

Acknowledgments

We would like to thank David Horton Smith for his helpful comments. Section 1 is based on our book *Understanding the social economy: A Canadian perspective*, 2nd edn (Quarter, Mook, & Armstrong, 2018), reprinted with permission of the publisher.

Bibliography

Akingbola, K. (2004). Government funding and staffing in the nonprofit sector. *Nonprofit Management and Leadership, 14*(4), 453–467.

Akingbola, K. (2013). Resource-based view (RBV) of unincorporated social economy organizations. *Canadian Journal of Nonprofit and Social Economy Research, 4*(1), 66–85.

Anderson, R. B., Dana, L. P., & Dana, T. E. (2006). Indigenous land rights, entrepreneurship, and economic development in Canada: "Opting-in" to the global economy. *Journal of World Business, 41*(1), 45–55.

Arsenault, G. (2018). Explaining Quebec's social economy turn. *Canadian Journal of Nonprofit and Social Economy Research, 9*(1), 58–75.

Behnia, B. (2012). Volunteering with newcomers: The perspectives of Canadian- and foreign-born volunteers. *Canadian Journal of Nonprofit and Social Economy Research, 3*(2), 6–23.

Ben-Ner, A. (1986). Non-profit organizations: Why do they exist in market economies? In S. Rose-Ackerman (Ed.), *The Economics of Nonprofit Institutions: Studies in Structure and Policy* (pp. 94–113). Oxford: Oxford University Press.

Billis, D. (Ed.) (2010). *Hybrid organizations and the third sector: Challenges for practice, theory and policy.* New York: Palgrave Macmillan.

Birchall, J. & Ketilson, L. H. (2009). *Resilience of the cooperative business model in times of crisis.* Geneva: International Labor Organization, Sustainable Enterprise Program.

Borzaga, C. & Defourny, J. (2001). *The emergence of social enterprise.* Andover: Routledge.

Borzaga, C. & Depedri, S. (2009). Working for social enterprises: Does it make a difference? In A. Amin (Ed.), *Social economy. International perspectives on economic solidarity* (pp. 82–114). London: Zed Press.

Bouchard, M. J. (2009). Methods and indicators for evaluating the social economy. In M. J. Bouchard (Ed.), *The worth of the social economy: An international perspective* (pp. 19–34). Brussels: P.I.E.-Peter Lang.

Bouchard, M. J. (Ed.) (2013). *Innovation and the social economy: The Quebec experience.* Toronto: University of Toronto Press.

Bouchard, M. J., Cruz Filho, P. & Zerdani, T. (2015). Social enterprise in Quebec: Understanding their "institutional footprint." *Canadian Journal of Nonprofit and Social Economy Research, 6*(1), 42–62.

Bradshaw, P. & Fredette, C. (2012). Determinants of the range of ethnocultural diversity on nonprofit boards: A study of large Canadian nonprofit organizations. *Nonprofit and Voluntary Sector Quarterly, 42*(6), 1111–1133.

Bradshaw, P., Murray, V., & Wolpin, J. (1996). Women on boards of nonprofits: What difference do they make? *Nonprofit Management and Leadership, 6*(3), 241–254.

Brouard, F., McMurtry, J. J., & Vieta, M. (2015). Social enterprise models in Canada-Ontario. *Canadian Journal of Nonprofit and Social Economy Research, 6*(1), 63–82.

Canada Revenue Agency (2015). Charitable purposes. Available at: http://www.cra-arc.gc.ca/chrts-gvng/chrts/pplyng/mdl/menu-eng.html (accessed October 31, 2015).

Carnegie, A. (1995 [1889]). *Wealth*. Available at: https://www.swarthmore.edu/SocSci/rbannis1/AIH19th/Carnegie.html (accessed October 31, 2015).

Carter, T. S., Hoffstein, M. E., & Parachin, A. (2016). *Charities, legislation and commentary*. Toronto: LexisNexis Canada.

CCA/BGI (Canadian Cooperative Association/Brown Governance Inc.) (2009). Counting on Canada's co-ops. Available at: https://www.governancesolutions.ca/governance-solutions/publications/pdfs/CountingonCanadasCoops.pdf (accessed September 23, 2018).

CCUA (Canadian Credit Union Association) (2016). Credit unions lead the way. Available at: https://ccua.com/credit_unions_in_canada/credit_unions_lead_the_way (accessed September 23, 2018).

CCUA (Canadian Credit Union Association) (2018a). Director training. Available at: https://www.ccua.com/cusource/director_training (accessed June 8, 2018).

CCUA (Canadian Credit Union Association) (2018b). National sector results: Fourth quarter 2017. Available at: https://www.ccua.com/~/media/CCUA/About/facts_and_figures/documents/Quarterly%20National%20System%20Results/4Q17SystemResults_14-Mar-18.pdf (accessed June 9, 2018).

CCUA (Canadian Credit Union Association) (2018c). National system results: Fourth quarter 2017. Available at: https://www.ccua.com/~/media/CCUA/About/facts_and_figures/documents/Quarterly%20National%20System%20Results/4Q17SystemResults_14-Mar-18.pdf (accessed June 20, 2018).

CHFT (Cooperative Housing Federation of Toronto) (2018). Staff education event. Available at: https://co-ophousingtoronto.coop/wp-content/uploads/2018/01/2staff-brochure.pdf (accessed June 8, 2018).

CIRIEC (2007). *The Social Economy in the European Union. Report No. CESE/COMM/05/2005*. Brussels: European Economic and Social Committee.

Cnaan, R. A., Handy, F. & Wadsworth, M. (1996). Defining who is a volunteer: Conceptual and empirical considerations. *Nonprofit and Voluntary Sector Quarterly, 25*(3), 364–383.

Community Foundations of Canada (2018a). Leadership development. Available at: http://communityfoundations.ca/foundation-development/leadership-development/ (accessed June 8, 2018).

Community Foundations of Canada (2018b). Vital signs. Available at: http://communityfoundations.ca/vitalsigns/reports/ (accessed June 26, 2018).

Conference Board of Canada (2018). *The value of volunteering in Canada*. Available at: https://volunteer.ca/vdemo/Campaigns_DOCS/Value%20of%20Volunteering%20

in%20Canada%20Conf%20Board%20Final%20Report%20EN.pdf (accessed October 8, 2018).

Co-op Canada (Cooperatives and Mutuals Canada) (2018). How to start a co-op. Available at: http://canada.coop/en/programs/co-op-development/how-start-co-op (accessed September 22, 2018).

Credit Union Institute (2018). Programs. Available at: https://www.dal.ca/faculty/cce/programs/credit-union-institute-of-canada-program.html (accessed June 8, 2018).

CSC (Centre for the Study of Cooperatives) (2018). About us. Available at: http://usaskstudies.coop/about-us/index.php (accessed June 9, 2018).

Defourny, J., Hulgård, L., & Pestoff, V. (Eds.). (2014). *Social enterprise and the third sector. Changing European landscapes in a comparative perspective*. London: Routledge.

Defourny, J. & Monzón Campos, J. L. (Eds.). (1992). *The third sector: Cooperative, mutual and nonprofit organizations*. Brussels: CIRIEC and DeBoeck University.

Devlin, R. A. & Zhao, W. (2017). Are Quebeckers really stingier than other Canadians? An empirical analysis of philanthropy in Canada and how Québec compares to other provinces. *Canadian Journal of Nonprofit and Social Economy Research, 8*(1), 20–39.

Diamantopoulos, M. (2011). Cooperative development gap in Quebec and Saskatchewan 1980 to 2010: A tale of two movements. *Canadian Journal of Nonprofit and Social Economy Research, 2*(2), 6–24.

Drayton, B. & Budinich, V. (2010). A new alliance for global change. *Harvard Business Review, 12*(5) (September), 56–64.

Eikenberry, A. M. & Kluver, J. D. (2004). The marketization of the nonprofit sector: Civil society at risk? *Public Administration Review, 64*(2), 132–140.

Einolf, C. J., Prouteau, L., Nezhina, T., & Ibrayeva, A. R. (2016). Informal, unorganized volunteering. In D. H. Smith, R. A. Stebbins and J. Grotz (Eds.), *The Palgrave handbook of volunteering, civic participation, and nonprofit associations* (pp. 223–241). New York: Palgrave Macmillan.

Ellerman, D. (1990). *The democratic worker-owned firm*. Boston, MA: Harper-Collins.

Elson, P. R., Fontan, J.-M., Lefèvre, S. & Stauch, J. (2018). Foundations in Canada: Comparative perspective. *American Behavioral Scientist, 62*(13), 1777–1802.

Elson, P. R., Hall, P., Leeson-Klym, S., Penner, D., & Andres, J. (2015). Social enterprises in the Canadian west. *Canadian Journal of Nonprofit and Social Economy Research, 6*(1), 83–103.

Elson, P. R., Hall, P., & Wamucii, P. (2016). *Canadian national social enterprise sector survey report*. Available at: http://sess.ca/wp-content/uploads/Canadian-National-Social-Enterprise-Sector-Survey-Report-2016.pdf (accessed July 27, 2018).

European Commission (2015). Social economy enterprises. Available at: http://ec.europa.eu/growth/smes/promoting-entrepreneurship/we-work-for/social-economy/index_en.htm (accessed June 25, 2018).

Favreau, L. (2006). Social economy and public policy: The Quebec experience. *Horizons, 8*(2), 7–15.

Fremont-Smith, M. R. (2004). *Governing nonprofit organizations: Federal and state law and regulation.* Cambridge, MA: Belknap Press of Harvard University.

Glass, J. & Pole, N. (2017). Collaboration between Canadian grantmaking foundations: The expression of an increasingly ambitious and strategic philanthropic sector? *Canadian Journal of Nonprofit and Social Economy Research, 8*(2), 57–79.

Government of Canada: Office of the Commissioner for Lobbying (2018). Coalition of National Voluntary Organizations (NVO). Available at: https://lobbycanada.gc.ca/app/secure/ocl/lrs/do/vwRg;jsessionid=FDu5SHMm-1nBx7TQddnMe43Z.app-ocl-01?regId=497242&cno=12186 (accessed June 20, 2018).

Hall, M. H., Barr, C., Easwaramoorthy, M., Sokolowski, S. W., & Salamon, L. M. (2005). *The Canadian nonprofit and voluntary sector in comparative perspective.* Toronto: Imagine Canada. Available at: http://sectorsource.ca/sites/default/files/resources/files/jhu_report_en.pdf (accessed June 8, 2018).

Hall, M., de Wit, M. L., Lasby, D., McIver, D., Evers, T., Johnson, C., McAuley, J., Cucumel, G., Jolin, L., Nicol, R., Berdahl, L., Roach, R., Davies, I., Rowe, P., Frankel, S., Brock, K., & Murray, V. (2005). *Cornerstones of community: Highlights of the national survey of nonprofit and voluntary organizations*, 2003 revised. (Catalogue No. 61–533-XPE, rev. edn.). Ottawa: Statistics Canada. Available at: http://www.imaginecanada.ca/sites/default/files/www/en/library/nsnvo/nsnvo_report_english.pdf (accessed June 18, 2018).

Hall, P. D. (1992). Conflicting managerial cultures in nonprofit organizations: Inventing the nonprofit sector and other essays on philanthropy, voluntarism, and nonprofit organizations. In P. D. Hall (Ed.), *Inventing the Nonprofit Sector and Other Essays on Philanthropy, Voluntarism, and Nonprofit Organizations* (pp. 207–220). Baltimore, MD: Johns Hopkins University Press.

Hall, P. D. (2005). Historical perspectives on nonprofit organizations in the United States. In D. Renz (Ed.), *The Jossey-Bass handbook of nonprofit leadership and management* (pp. 3–38). New York: Wiley.

Hancock, E. & Brault, A. (2016). *The fifth cooperative principle in action: Mapping the cooperative educational initiatives of Canadian cooperatives.* Saskatoon: Centre for the Study of Cooperatives.

Hansmann, H. B. (1980). The role of nonprofit enterprise. *Yale Law Journal, 89*(5), 835–901.

Hansmann, H. B. (1996). *The ownership of enterprise.* Cambridge, MA: Harvard University Press.

Heneberry, J. & Laforest, R. (2011). Cooperatives and the state: The case of Ontario. *Canadian Journal of Nonprofit and Social Economy Research, 2*(2), 57–70.

Hopkins, B. R. (1987). *The law of tax-exempt organizations* (5th edn). New York: Wiley.

Hossein, C. S. (2013). The black social economy: Perseverance of banker ladies in the slums. *Annals of Public and Cooperative Economics, 84*(4), 423–442.

Hossein, C. S. (2014a). The politics of resistance: Informal banks in the Caribbean. *Review of Black Political Economy, 41*(1), 85–100.

Hossein, C. S. (2014b). Haiti's *caisses populaires*: Home-grown solutions to bring economic democracy. *International Journal of Social Economics, 41*(1), 42–59.

Hossein, C. S. (2016). *Politicized microfinance: Money, power, and violence in the black Americas*. Toronto: University of Toronto Press.

Hossein, C. S. (2017). Fringe banking in Canada: A study of rotating savings and credit associations (ROSCAs) in Toronto's inner suburbs. *Canadian Journal of Nonprofit and Social Economy Research, 8*(1), 5–19.

ICA (International Cooperative Alliance) (2018). Cooperative identity, values & principles. Available at: https://www.ica.coop/en/whats-co-op/cooperative-identity-values-principles (accessed September 22, 2018).

Imagine Canada (2014). Scope of the sector. Available at: http://sectorsource.ca/sites/default/files/resources/files/narrative-issue-sheet-scope-en.pdf (accessed October 10, 2018).

Imagine Canada (2018). Standards program. Available at: http://www.imaginecanada.ca/our-programs/standards-program (accessed June 8, 2018).

Industry Canada (2018). 2013: Cooperatives in Canada. Ottawa: Minister of Innovation, Science and Economic Development Canada. Available at: https://www.ic.gc.ca/eic/site/061.nsf/vwapj/Coop_in_Canada_2013_eng-V2.pdf/$file/Coop_in_Canada_2013_eng-V2.pdf (accessed June 9, 2018).

Kirk, S. A. & Reid, W. J. (2002). *Science and social work: A critical appraisal*. New York: Columbia University Press.

Kropotkin, P. (1989 [1902]). *Mutual aid: A factor in evolution*. Montreal: Black Rose.

Larre, T. (2016). Allowing charities to "do more good" through carrying on unrelated businesses. *Canadian Journal of Nonprofit and Social Economy Research, 7*(1), 29–45.

Lionais, D. (2015). Social enterprise in Atlantic Canada. *Canadian Journal of Nonprofit and Social Economy Research, 6*(1), 25–41.

Liston-Heyes, C., Hall, P. V., Jevtovic, N., & Elson, P. R. (2017). Canadian social enterprises: Who gets the non-earned income? *Voluntas, 28*(6), 2546–2568.

Livingstone, D. (1999). Exploring the icebergs of adult learning: Findings of the first Canadian survey of informal learning practices. *Canadian Journal for the Study of Adult Education, 3*, 49–72.

Loewenberg, F. M. (2001). *From charity to social justice: The emergence of communal institutions for the support of the poor in ancient Judaism*. New Brunswick, NJ: Transaction Publishers.

Loomis, C. J. (2010). The $600 billion challenge. *Fortune* (June 16). Available at: http://fortune.com/2010/06/16/ (accessed March 30, 2015).

MacPherson, I. (1979). *Each for all: A history of the cooperative movement in English Canada, 1900–1945.* Toronto: Macmillan.

MacPherson, I. (1999). *Hands around the globe: A history of the international credit union movement and the role and development of the world council of credit union.* Madison, WI: World Council of Credit Unions.

McMurtry, J. J. (Ed.) (2010). Introducing the social economy in theory and practice. In J. J. McMurtry (Ed.). *Living economics: Canadian perspectives on the social economy, co-operatives, and community economic development* (pp. 1–34). Toronto: Emond Montgomery Press.

McMurtry, J. J., and Brouard, F. (2015). Social enterprises in Canada: An introduction. *Canadian Journal of Nonprofit and Social Economy Research, 6*(1), 6–17.

Maiorano, J., Mook, L., and Quarter, J. (2016). Is there a credit union difference? Comparing credit union and bank branch locations. *Canadian Journal of Nonprofit and Social Economy Research, 7*(1), 40–56.

MaRS Centre for Impact Investing (2016). Certified B corporation. Available at: http://impactinvesting.marsdd.com/strategic-initiatives/benefit-corporation-b-corp-hub/ (accessed May 4, 2016).

Martin, S. A. (1985). *An essential grace: Funding Canada's health care, education, welfare, religion, and culture.* Toronto: McClelland and Stewart.

Martin, R. & Osberg, S. (2015). *Getting beyond better: How social entrepreneurship works.* Cambridge, MA: Harvard University Review Press.

Mendell, M. & Neamtan, N. (2010). The social economy in Quebec: Towards a new political economy. In Jack Quarter, Laurie Mook, and Sherida Ryan (Eds.) *Researching the social economy* (pp. 63–82). Toronto: University of Toronto Press.

Mendell, M. & Rouzier, R. (2006). Some initiatives that enabled the institutionalization of Quebec's social economy: Civil society's crucial role and the state's essential role. Montreal: Concordia University, Unpublished document.

Monzón Campos, J. L. & Chaves, R. (2012). The social economy in the European union. Available at: https://www.eesc.europa.eu/resources/docs/qe-30-12-790-en-c.pdf (accessed May 4, 2016).

Mook, L. (2013). Social accounting for the social economy. In L. Mook (Ed.), *Accounting for social value* (pp. 5–28). Toronto: University of Toronto Press.

Mook, L., Hann, J., & Quarter, J. (2012). Understanding the rural tilt among financial cooperatives in Canada. *Canadian Journal of Nonprofit and Social Economy Research, 3*(1), 42–58.

Mook, L., Quarter, J., & Richmond, B. J. (2007). *What counts: Social accounting for nonprofits and cooperatives* (2nd edn.). London: Sigel Press.

Mook, L. & Theriault, L. (2018). Ten years of ANSER-ARES conferences: Discussion paper prepared for the 2018 ANSER-ARES conference, University of Regina, May 31.

North, D. C. (2005 [1990]). *Institutions, Institutional Change and Economic Performance.* New York: Cambridge University Press.

Novkovic, S. (2008). Defining the cooperative difference. *The Journal of Socio-Economics, 37*(6), 2168–2177.

Novkovic, S. & Gordon Nembhard, J. (2017). Beyond the economy: The social impact of cooperatives. *The Cooperative Business Journal,* (Fall), 12–22.

Pestoff, V. A. (1998). *Between market and state: Social enterprise and civil democracy in a welfare society.* Aldershot: Ashgate.

Philanthropic Foundations Canada (2018). Overview of the foundation sector. Available at: https://pfc.ca/resources/canadian-foundation-facts/ (accessed October 6, 2018).

Philanthropist Editors (2000). The founding of the Canadian Centre for Philanthropy. Available at: https://thephilanthropist.ca/2000/01/the-founding-of-the-canadian-\-for-philanthropy/ (accessed June 20, 2018).

Prahalad, C. K. & Hammond, A. (2002). Serving the world's poor profitably. *Harvard Business Review, 80*(9), 48–57.

Quarter, J., Mook, L., & Armstrong, A. (2009). *Understanding the social economy: A Canadian perspective,* 1st edn. Toronto: University of Toronto Press.

Quarter, J., Mook, L., & Armstrong, A. (2018). *Understanding the social economy: A Canadian perspective,* 2nd edn. Toronto: University of Toronto Press.

Reed, P. B. & Selbee, L. K. (2001). Volunteering and giving: A regional perspective. Canadian Social Trends. Ottawa: Statistics Canada: Catalogue No. 11–008. Available at: https://www150.statcan.gc.ca/n1/en/pub/11–008-x/2001003/article/6006-eng.pdf?st=GxViYssD.

Restoule, J.-P., Gruner, S., & Metatawabin, E. (2012). Land, self-determination and the social economy in Fort Albany first nation. In L. Mook, J. Quarter, & S. Ryan (Eds.), *Businesses with a difference: Balancing the social and economic* (pp. 182–201). Toronto: University of Toronto Press.

Rifkin, J. (2014). *The zero marginal cost society.* New York: Palgrave Macmillan.

Robbins, K. C. (2006). The nonprofit sector in historical perspective: Traditions of philanthropy in the west. In W. W. Powell & R. Steinberg (Eds.), *The nonprofit sector: A research handbook* (pp. 13–31). New Haven, CT: Yale University Press.

Salamon, L. M. (1987). Partners in public service: The scope and theory of government–nonprofit relations. In W. W. Powell (Ed.), *The nonprofit sector: A research handbook* (pp. 99–117). New Haven, CT: Yale University Press.

Salamon, L. M. (1995). *Partners in public service: Government–nonprofit relations in the modern welfare state.* Baltimore, MD: Johns Hopkins University Press.

Salamon, L. M. & Anheier, H. K. (1997). *Defining the nonprofit sector: A cross-national analysis*. Manchester: Manchester University Press.

Salamon, L. M., Anheier, H., List, R., Toepler, S., Sokolowski, S. W., & Associates. (1999). *Global civil society: Dimensions of the nonprofit sector*. Baltimore, MD: Johns Hopkins University Press.

Schugurensky, D. (2000). *The forms of informal learning: Towards a conceptualization of the field*. Working Paper 19–2000. Available at: https://tspace.library.utoronto.ca/bitstream/1807/2733/2/19formsofinformal.pdf (accessed December 8, 2018).

Sengupta, U. (2015). The intersection of race and gender in leadership of cooperatives: of whom, by whom and for whom? *Journal of Cooperative Studies, 48*(3), 19–28.

Sengupta, U., Vieta, M., & McMurtry, J. J. (2015). Indigenous communities and social enterprises in Canada: Incorporating culture as an essential ingredient of entrepreneurship. *Canadian Journal of Nonprofit and Social Economy Research, 6*(1), 103–123.

SEOntario (2018). Government of Ontario support for social enterprise. Available at: https://seontario.org/home/about-social-enterprise-ontario/government-of-ontario-support-for-social-enterprise/ (accessed October 7, 2018).

Shier, M. & Handy, F. (2014). Research trends in nonprofit graduate studies: A growing interdisciplinary field. *Nonprofit and Voluntary Sector Quarterly, 43*(5), 812–831.

Shragge, E. & Fontan, J.-M. (Eds.). (2000). Introduction. In E. Shragge and J.-M. Fontan (Eds.), *Social economy: International debates and perspectives* (pp. 1–21). Montreal: Black Rose.

Sinha, M. (2015). Volunteering in Canada, 2004 to 2013. Ottawa: Statistics Canada. Available at: https://www150.statcan.gc.ca/n1/en/pub/89-652-x/89-652-x2015003-eng.pdf?st=aqC3ZqJt (accessed December 8, 2018).

Small Business BC (2015). Top 5 Questions About BC's New "Community Contribution Company" Answered. Available at: https://smallbusinessbc.ca/article/top-5-questions-about-bcs-new-community-contribution-company-answered/ (accessed December 8, 2018).

Smith, D. H. (1997a). The rest of the nonprofit sector: Grassroots associations as the dark matter ignored in prevailing "flat-earth" maps of the sector. *Nonprofit and Voluntary Sector Quarterly, 26*(2), 114–131.

Smith, D. H. (1997b). Grassroots associations are important: Some theory and a review of the impact literature. *Nonprofit and Voluntary Sector Quarterly, 26*(3), 269–306.

Smith, D. H. (2006). The current state of civil society and volunteering in the world, the USA, and China. *China Nonprofit Review, 6*(1), 137–150.

Smith, D. H. (2013). Growth of research associations and journals in the emerging discipline of altruistics. *Nonprofit and Voluntary Sector Quarterly, 42*(4), 638–656.

Smith, D. H. (2016). A survey of voluntaristics: Research on the growth of the global, interdisciplinary, socio-behavioral science field and emergent inter-discipline. *Voluntaristics Review, 1*(2), 1–81.

Smith, K., Holmes, K., Haski Leventhal, D., Cnaan, R. A., Handy, F., & Brudney, J. L. (2010). Motivations and benefits of student volunteering: Comparing regular, occasional, and non-volunteers in five countries. *Canadian Journal of Nonprofit and Social Economy Research, 1*(1), 65–81.

Smith, S. R. & Lipsky, M. (1993). *Non-profits for hire: The welfare state in the age of contracting.* Cambridge, MA: Harvard University Press.

Spear, R. (2010). The social economy in Europe: Trends and challenges. In J. Quarter, L. Mook, & S. Ryan (Eds.), *Researching the social economy* (pp. 84–105). Toronto: University of Toronto Press.

Speevak Sladowski, P. & Kaleniecka, J. (2014). *Employer-supported volunteering: The practice and promise of community engagement.* Ottawa: Volunteer Canada. Available at: https://volunteer.ca/vdemo/EngagingVolunteers_DOCS/ESV%20Primer%20 Full%20Report.pdf (accessed October 8, 2018).

SSES (Social and Solidarity Economy Summit) (2006). 2006 Declaration. Presented at the conclusion of the social and solidarity economy summit held in Montréal. Available at: http://www.chantier.qc.ca/userImgs/documents/ (accessed May 8, 2018).

SSHRC (Social Sciences and Humanities Research Council of Canada) (2018). Facts and figures. Available at: http://www.sshrc-crsh.gc.ca/about-au_sujet/facts-faits/index -eng.aspx (accessed June 26, 2018).

Statistics Canada (2016). Immigration and Ethnocultural Diversity in Canada. Ottawa: Author. Available at: https://www12.statcan.gc.ca/nhs-enm/2011/as-sa/99-010-x/99 -010-x2011001-eng.cfm#a4 (accessed May 18, 2018).

Statistics Canada (2017a). Ethnic and cultural origins of Canadians: Portrait of a rich heritage. Ottawa: Author. Available at: http://www12.statcan.gc.ca/census -recensement/2016/as-sa/98-200-x/2016016/98-200-x2016016-eng.cfm (accessed May 18, 2018).

Statistics Canada (2017b). 2016 Census: 150 years of urbanization in Canada. Catalogue number: Catalogue number:11-629-x [video]. Ottawa: Author. Available at: http://www.statcan.gc.ca/eng/sc/video/2016census_150yearsurbanization (accessed May 18, 2018).

Sulek, M. & Mirabella, R. (forthcoming, 2019). Nonprofit management education in Canada. *Journal of Nonprofit Education and Leadership.*

The Circle (2018). Supporters/directory. Available at: http://www.philanthropyandab originalpeoples.ca/why-join/directory/ (accessed October 6, 2018).

Thériault, L. (2014). Exploring 50 years of Canadian theses on cooperatives. *Journal of Cooperative Studies, 47*(1), 56–70.

Thompson, M. & Emmanuel, J. (2012). *Assembling understandings: Findings from the Canadian social economy research partnerships, 2005–2011.* Victoria: University of Victoria.

Turcotte, M. (2015a). Spotlight on Canadians: Results from the general social survey: Volunteering and charitable giving in Canada. Available at: https://www150.statcan .gc.ca/n1/en/pub/89-652-x/89-652-x2015001-eng.pdf?st=vop6UY8t (accessed August 16, 2018).

Turcotte, M. (2015b). Spotlight on Canadians: Results from the general social survey: Charitable giving by individuals. Available at: https://www150.statcan.gc.ca/n1/en/ pub/89-652-x/89-652-x2015008-eng.pdf?st=QF_gLecq (accessed August 26, 2018).

Turcotte, M. (2015c). Spotlight on Canadians: Results from the general social survey: Civic engagement and political participation in Canada. Available at: https:// www150.statcan.gc.ca/n1/en/pub/89-652-x/89-652-x2015006-eng.pdf?st=yymotbtb (accessed August 24, 2018).

United Nations (2018). Satellite account on nonprofit and related institutions and volunteer work, final draft. Available at: http://ccss.jhu.edu/wp-content/uploads/ downloads/2018/10/UN_TSE_HB_FNL_web.pdf (accessed October 9, 2018).

Vieta, M., Quarter, J., Spear, R., & Moskovskaya, A. (2016). Participation in worker cooperatives. In D. Horton Smith, R. A. Stebbins, & J. Grotz (Eds.), *The Palgrave handbook of volunteering, civic participation, and nonprofit associations* (pp. 436–453). New York: Palgrave Macmillan.

Volunteer Canada (2016). Leading with intention: Employer-supported volunteering in Canada. Ottawa: Volunteer Canada. Available at: https://volunteer.ca/vdemo/ EngagingVolunteers_DOCS/LeadingwithIntentionEN.pdf (accessed October 8, 2018).

Wang, L., Mook, L., & Handy, F. (2017). An empirical examination of formal and informal volunteering in Canada. *Voluntas, 28*(1), 139–161.

Weisbrod, B. (1975). Toward a theory of the voluntary non-profit sector in a three-sector economy. In E. Phelps (Ed.), *Altruism, Morality and Economic Theory* (pp. 171–195). New York: Russell Sage.

Weisbrod, B. (1977). *The Voluntary Non-Profit Sector*. Lexington, MA: D.C. Heath.

World Atlas (2018). The most cosmopolitan cities in the world. Available at: https:// www.worldatlas.com/articles/the-most-cosmopolitan-cities-in-the-world.html (accessed December 8, 2018).

Wuttunee, W. (2010). Aboriginal perspectives on the social economy. In J. J. McMurtry (Ed.), *Living economics: Canadian perspectives on the social economy, cooperatives, and community economic development* (pp. 179–216). Toronto: Emond Montgomery.

Yunus, M. (2010). *Building social business: The new kind of capitalism that serves humanity's most pressing needs*. New York: Public Affairs.

Author Biographies

Laurie Mook

Laurie Mook is Associate Professor in the School of Community Resources and Development, and research associate at the Lodestar Center for Philanthropy and Nonprofit Innovation, at Arizona State University. She received her Ph.D. from the University of Toronto. Dr. Mook's areas of interest are the social economy (nonprofits, cooperatives, and social enterprises), social accounting, and volunteerism. Prior to moving to Arizona, Dr. Mook was co-director of the Social Economy Centre at the University of Toronto in Canada. She is a founding member of the *Association for Nonprofit and Social Economy Research* (ANSER) and serves on its executive board.

Dr. Mook is co-author of *What counts: Social accounting for nonprofits and cooperatives* (second edition from Sigel Press), *Understanding the social economy: A Canadian perspective* (now in its second edition), and *Understanding the social economy of the United States* (both from the University of Toronto Press). She is editor of *Accounting for social value* and co-editor of *Businesses with a difference: Balancing the social and the economic* and *Researching the social economy*, all published by the University of Toronto Press. She is also the author of many journal articles and book chapters.

Jack Quarter

Jack Quarter is a professor at the University of Toronto, Department of Leadership, Higher and Adult Education, in the Ontario Institute for Studies in Education. He received his Ph.D. from the University of Toronto. Professor Quarter is best known for his writing and research on Canada's social economy, and especially the study of work integration social enterprises. His recent books include: *Understanding the social economy: A Canadian perspective*, with Laurie Mook and Ann Armstrong (2nd edition, 2018); *Understanding the social economy of the United States*, with Laurie Mook, John Whitman, and Ann Armstrong (2015); *Social purpose enterprises: Case studies for social change*, with Sherida Ryan and Andrea Chan (2015); *Business with a difference: Balancing the social and economic*, with Laurie Mook and Sherida Ryan (2012); and *Researching the social economy*, also with Laurie Mook and Sherida Ryan (2010) (all University of Toronto Press).

Professor Quarter was one of the founders of the *Association for Nonprofit and Social Economy Research* (ANSER), a pan-Canadian association for nonprofits, cooperatives, and the social economy, and was its founding president from 2008 to 2014. He received the Distinguished Service Award from ANSER in 2015. He was also a founder of the Social Economy Centre at the University of Toronto, now the Centre for Learning, Social Economy, and Work. Previously, he helped to organize the Canadian Worker

Co-operative Federation. His PhD supervisees can be found in faculty positions at universities and colleges throughout Canada and the USA—something of which he is very proud. He has been very successful in funding competitions through the Social Sciences and Humanities Research Council of Canada, the main funding body for the humanities and social sciences in Canada.